The Internet of Things (IoT) Handbook

Connecting the World Understand IoT applications, architecture, and implementation strategies

THOMPSON CARTER

Table of Content

TABLE OF CONTENTS

Introduction

The **Internet of Things (IoT)** has transitioned from a concept of the future to a key driver of innovation in the present day. Today, IoT is seamlessly integrated into our everyday lives—connecting devices, systems, and services in ways that were once unimaginable. Whether it's a smart thermostat adjusting the temperature in your home, a wearable device tracking your health, or a factory using sensors to monitor and optimize production, IoT is reshaping industries, businesses, and even how we live.

However, as with any transformative technology, the Internet of Things presents not only incredible opportunities but also significant challenges. The sheer number of connected devices and the vast amounts of data they generate make designing, implementing, and managing IoT solutions a complex task. From **network connectivity** and **data security** to **privacy concerns** and **scalability**, there are many factors that need to be considered to ensure that IoT systems are secure, efficient, and effective.

This book, **"The Internet of Things (IoT) Handbook: Connecting the World"**, is designed to guide readers through the essential concepts, technologies, and real-world applications of IoT. Whether you are a beginner exploring the world of IoT or an experienced professional looking to deepen your understanding, this comprehensive guide will provide valuable insights into the IoT ecosystem.

Why This Book?

The primary goal of this book is to make the intricate world of IoT accessible to everyone, regardless of their technical background. We understand that IoT can be overwhelming, given its complexity and wide-reaching implications across various sectors, from **smart homes** and **healthcare** to **manufacturing** and **agriculture**. This book breaks down the key components of IoT, demystifies the technology behind it, and highlights its potential for creating innovative solutions that can solve some of the world's most pressing problems.

From a **business perspective**, we'll explore how IoT is driving new business models, offering opportunities for data monetization, and creating recurring revenue streams through subscription-based services. We'll also delve into how **IoT is revolutionizing industries**, enabling smarter cities, more efficient factories, personalized healthcare, and much more.

As **IoT professionals**, understanding the foundational concepts of **device connectivity**, **network protocols**, **data analytics**, and **security** is essential. But it's also crucial to grasp how these technologies intersect with **emerging innovations** like **5G**, **artificial intelligence (AI)**, and **edge computing** to push the boundaries of what's possible. This book will guide you through the practical, real-world implications of these advancements and provide you with the knowledge needed to navigate and leverage these innovations effectively.

Key Focus Areas of This Book:

1. **IoT Fundamentals**: We'll begin by laying a solid foundation with an introduction to IoT, explaining its components, architecture, and the crucial role of **sensors**, **actuators**, **connectivity protocols**, and **cloud/edge computing** in creating connected solutions.

2. **Applications and Use Cases**: From **smart homes** to **smart cities**, **healthcare**, **manufacturing**, and **transportation**, we will examine how IoT is driving change across various sectors, improving efficiency, reducing costs, and enhancing customer experiences.

3. **Security and Privacy**: IoT brings new security challenges, including the risk of unauthorized access, data breaches, and misuse of personal information. We'll discuss the **ethical concerns** surrounding IoT data collection, data protection laws like **GDPR**, and best practices for securing IoT systems.

4. **Business Models and Innovation**: This book will explore the various business models around IoT solutions, such as **Product-as-a-Service (PaaS)**, **IoT as a Service (IoTaaS)**, and **data monetization**. We'll explore real-world case studies and discuss how businesses are leveraging IoT to innovate, improve operational efficiency, and create new revenue streams.

5. **The Future of IoT**: We'll conclude by looking ahead to the future of IoT, focusing on emerging technologies like **5G**, **AI**, and **blockchain**, and how they will impact the next generation of IoT solutions. We'll also discuss predictions for the next decade, where IoT will continue to shape our world in ways we are only beginning to understand.

Who Is This Book For?

This book is designed for a wide audience. Whether you're a **beginner** just starting to explore IoT or an **experienced professional** seeking to deepen your knowledge, this guide offers something for everyone. It's also useful for **business leaders**, **entrepreneurs**, and **product managers** looking to understand how to integrate IoT into their strategies and offerings. Moreover, **students** and **engineers** will find valuable technical insights that help them build, develop, and deploy IoT solutions.

- **Beginners** will find simple, clear explanations of complex concepts, making IoT approachable and easy to understand.
- **Professionals** will gain insights into IoT's evolving landscape, learning how it impacts business operations and the tech industry.
- **Entrepreneurs** will discover innovative business models and successful real-world IoT applications.
- **Technologists** and **engineers** will benefit from practical guidance on the tools, platforms, and technologies used in building IoT systems.

Why Now?

The IoT revolution is happening right now, and it's impacting every industry, from agriculture to urban development, healthcare to logistics, manufacturing to entertainment. The opportunity to leverage IoT for innovation and efficiency is enormous, and the demand for skilled professionals is rapidly growing. As we move into a more connected world, the importance of understanding IoT's potential and how to build IoT solutions will be key to staying competitive and relevant in the evolving technology landscape.

This book serves as both a comprehensive introduction and a practical guide for anyone looking to understand the current state and future of IoT. Whether you are involved in developing IoT products, managing IoT-based businesses, or simply exploring the concept, this book will provide the foundational knowledge and forward-thinking insights necessary to thrive in the IoT-driven world.

Welcome to the world of the **Internet of Things**—a world that is transforming the way we live, work, and interact with the world around us. Let's dive in and begin this exciting journey of understanding how IoT is connecting the world and shaping our future.

CHAPTER 1

INTRODUCTION TO IOT

Overview of the Internet of Things (IoT)

The Internet of Things (IoT) refers to a network of physical objects or "things" that are embedded with sensors, software, and other technologies, enabling them to connect and exchange data with each other over the internet. These "things" can range from everyday household items like refrigerators and light bulbs to more complex systems like industrial machinery or medical devices. Essentially, IoT enables the communication of devices, allowing them to collect, transmit, and analyze data autonomously, providing smart capabilities to traditionally non-smart objects.

In its simplest form, IoT connects devices to the internet to exchange data and improve efficiencies. For example, a smart thermostat can communicate with your heating system to adjust room temperature based on your preferences or the weather outside.

The Evolution of IoT

The concept of connected devices isn't new, but the development of IoT as we know it today began with the rise of the internet in the late 1990s. Early versions of IoT were primarily used in industrial settings where devices communicated via basic network protocols to optimize processes. The term "Internet of Things" was first coined by Kevin Ashton in 1999, as he envisioned a world where the physical and digital realms could seamlessly interact through connected devices.

The early 2000s saw the emergence of RFID (Radio Frequency Identification) technology, which enabled passive devices to communicate and transmit data to readers. However, it wasn't until the growth of wireless internet, advancements in low-cost sensors, and the ubiquity of cloud computing that IoT truly began to take off.

By the 2010s, with the explosion of smartphones, Wi-Fi, and Bluetooth technologies, the IoT ecosystem began to grow exponentially, making it easier and cheaper to create connected devices. Today, the rapid adoption of 5G networks, improved AI capabilities, and the increased use of edge computing has propelled IoT even further, enabling faster communication and smarter decision-making in real-time.

Real-World Examples of IoT Applications

- **Smart Homes:** Smart homes are among the most visible IoT applications today. Devices like smart thermostats (e.g., Nest), lighting systems (e.g., Philips Hue), and security cameras (e.g., Ring) allow homeowners to control and monitor their homes remotely. These devices can be programmed to learn preferences, automatically adjust settings, and provide real-time alerts to homeowners, all through smartphone apps.

- **Healthcare:** IoT is revolutionizing healthcare by enabling remote monitoring and improving patient care. Wearable devices like Fitbit or Apple Watch track health metrics such as heart rate, sleep patterns, and physical activity, providing valuable data that can help prevent health issues. In hospitals, IoT-enabled medical devices, such as connected pacemakers, can relay data to doctors, ensuring timely interventions.

- **Agriculture:** In agriculture, IoT sensors can monitor soil moisture, temperature, and weather conditions, allowing farmers to optimize irrigation and increase crop yields. For example, John Deere's smart tractors collect data that helps farmers make data-driven decisions on how to plant, irrigate, and harvest crops.

- **Industrial IoT (IIoT):** In manufacturing, IoT is used to improve efficiency and reduce downtime through predictive maintenance. Sensors embedded in machines monitor performance and send alerts when equipment is at risk of failure. This allows businesses to address issues before they cause breakdowns, saving costs on repairs and reducing unplanned downtime.

- **Smart Cities:** IoT plays a crucial role in the development of smart cities, where technology is used to optimize urban life. Traffic management systems use IoT sensors to track vehicle flow, reduce congestion, and improve safety. IoT-enabled waste management systems monitor waste levels in trash bins and optimize collection schedules, leading to more efficient waste disposal.

These examples showcase how IoT is transforming various industries by enhancing efficiency, improving convenience, and providing real-time insights. As IoT continues to evolve, its applications will become even more widespread, creating smarter, more connected environments across the globe.

This chapter serves as the foundation for understanding IoT, providing a clear picture of its significance, evolution, and diverse applications. Would you like to delve into more examples or explore any specific aspect further?

CHAPTER 2

THE IOT LANDSCAPE

Key Players in the IoT Ecosystem

The Internet of Things (IoT) ecosystem is vast and multifaceted, consisting of several key players that enable the growth and functionality of IoT systems. These players are responsible for designing, building, and supporting IoT solutions across various industries. Some of the key players in the IoT ecosystem include:

1. **Device Manufacturers:** These are the companies that design and manufacture the physical IoT devices, such as sensors, wearables, smart home devices, and industrial equipment. Major players include:
   - **Samsung**: Known for its smart home appliances and wearable devices.
   - **Nest (a subsidiary of Google)**: Specializes in smart thermostats and smoke detectors.
   - **Bosch**: A key player in industrial IoT, providing sensors and IoT-enabled solutions for manufacturing.

2. **Network Providers:** IoT devices rely on connectivity to send and receive data. Network providers facilitate the communication between devices, either through wireless technologies like Wi-Fi, 5G, and Bluetooth or through cellular networks. Leading network providers include:

   o **Verizon**: Offers 5G and IoT connectivity solutions for enterprises.

   o **AT&T**: A major player in providing IoT connectivity through cellular and low-power wide-area networks (LPWAN).

   o **T-Mobile**: Provides IoT connectivity through 5G networks, supporting applications like connected cars and smart cities.

3. **Platform Providers:** These companies offer IoT platforms that help manage, analyze, and secure IoT devices. They provide software that enables seamless communication and data processing. Notable platform providers include:

   o **Microsoft Azure IoT**: Provides cloud-based solutions for managing IoT devices and processing data.

   o **Amazon Web Services (AWS) IoT**: Offers a comprehensive suite of tools to connect, monitor, and manage IoT devices.

o **Google Cloud IoT**: A platform that helps businesses integrate IoT devices with Google's powerful cloud infrastructure for data analysis.

4. **System Integrators and Application Developers:** These players help businesses integrate IoT technologies into their existing operations. They work with IoT hardware and software to create customized solutions for clients. Major players include:

   o **Accenture**: Provides IoT consulting and integration services for industries ranging from manufacturing to healthcare.

   o **IBM**: Known for its Watson IoT platform, IBM works with businesses to develop IoT applications and AI-driven insights.

5. **Data Analytics Providers:** Companies specializing in IoT data analytics offer tools that help businesses analyze and derive actionable insights from the massive volumes of data generated by IoT devices. Leading data analytics providers include:

   o **Palantir**: A data analytics company that helps organizations analyze and visualize IoT data.

   o **SAP**: Offers IoT solutions and analytics to help businesses manage and optimize their operations.

6. **Security Providers:** Given the vast amount of data generated by IoT devices, securing this data is a critical aspect of IoT systems. Security companies specialize in protecting IoT devices and networks from cyber threats. Examples include:

   o **McAfee**: Offers security solutions specifically designed to protect IoT devices.

   o **Symantec**: Provides IoT security services to ensure data protection and privacy.

IoT Industries and Verticals

IoT is transforming numerous industries by improving efficiencies, automating processes, and creating new business models. Below are some of the key industries and verticals where IoT is making a significant impact:

1. **Smart Homes:** IoT-enabled devices in smart homes, such as thermostats, lighting systems, and security cameras, are helping homeowners control and monitor their environments remotely. This vertical is growing rapidly, driven by the increasing adoption of voice assistants like Amazon Alexa and Google Assistant.

2. **Healthcare:** In healthcare, IoT is used for remote patient monitoring, smart medical devices, and

20

improving hospital management systems. Wearable devices like fitness trackers and medical sensors help doctors and patients monitor health metrics, while connected devices enable remote consultations and treatments.

3. **Automotive:** The automotive industry is adopting IoT technologies for connected vehicles, smart traffic management, and autonomous driving. IoT-enabled vehicles collect data on driving habits, performance, and maintenance needs, enhancing safety, convenience, and efficiency.

4. **Industrial IoT (IIoT):** Industrial IoT is transforming manufacturing and supply chain management. Sensors on machinery collect data on performance, helping businesses predict failures before they occur, reduce downtime, and optimize production lines. IIoT also enhances logistics by tracking goods in transit.

5. **Agriculture:** IoT is being used in agriculture to monitor soil moisture, temperature, and crop health. Smart farming solutions enable farmers to optimize irrigation, automate machinery, and improve crop yield predictions, leading to more sustainable and efficient agricultural practices.

6. **Retail:** In retail, IoT technologies help businesses manage inventory, optimize supply chains, and personalize customer experiences. Smart shelves and connected point-of-sale systems provide valuable insights into shopping behavior and product demand.

7. **Energy and Utilities:** IoT is used in energy management systems to optimize energy consumption, monitor grid health, and enable predictive maintenance. Smart meters and IoT-enabled grids help utilities manage energy distribution and detect faults in real-time.

8. **Smart Cities:** IoT is a cornerstone of smart city development, enabling the creation of more sustainable, efficient, and livable urban environments. IoT applications in smart cities include intelligent traffic systems, waste management, and energy-efficient buildings.

Market Trends and Forecasts

The IoT market has grown significantly in recent years, and its potential is immense. Below are some of the key trends and market forecasts that demonstrate the future of IoT:

1. **Expansion of IoT Devices:** The number of connected devices is expected to reach tens of billions in the coming years. According to Statista, the number of IoT devices is forecast to exceed 30 billion by 2025. This rapid growth is driven by advancements in wireless communication, lower-cost sensors, and the increasing demand for connected devices across various industries.

2. **Rise of 5G Connectivity:** The rollout of 5G networks is expected to significantly boost IoT adoption. 5G offers faster speeds, lower latency, and more reliable connections, making it ideal for supporting the vast number of IoT devices that require constant communication. 5G is particularly beneficial for real-time IoT applications such as autonomous vehicles and industrial automation.

3. **AI and Machine Learning Integration:** As IoT devices generate vast amounts of data, AI and machine learning will play a crucial role in analyzing this data and providing actionable insights. The integration of AI into IoT systems will enable automation, predictive maintenance, and intelligent decision-making in real-time.

4. **IoT Security and Privacy:** As IoT adoption grows, so does the risk of cyberattacks and data breaches. Companies are increasingly focusing on IoT security to protect devices and networks from vulnerabilities. The demand for IoT security solutions is expected to rise as businesses prioritize securing their connected ecosystems.

5. **IoT in Healthcare:** The healthcare industry is expected to see significant growth in IoT applications, particularly in telemedicine, wearable health devices, and remote patient monitoring. The COVID-19 pandemic accelerated the adoption of IoT in healthcare, and this trend is expected to continue as the healthcare system becomes more reliant on connected devices.

6. **Edge Computing:** Edge computing, where data processing occurs closer to the source of data generation (such as IoT devices), is gaining traction as it reduces latency and bandwidth requirements. The demand for edge computing is expected to grow as IoT devices require faster, real-time data processing.

7. **IoT Monetization:** With the increase in IoT adoption, businesses are finding new ways to

monetize IoT data. Companies are exploring subscription models, data-driven services, and IoT-enabled products as new revenue streams.

This chapter introduces the IoT landscape, providing an understanding of key players, industry applications, and future trends. The insights into these aspects help readers grasp how IoT is shaping industries and the world around us. Would you like to explore any of these sections in more detail?

CHAPTER 3

COMPONENTS OF IOT

Sensors, Actuators, and Devices

In an IoT system, the core components are sensors, actuators, and devices. These components are responsible for collecting, processing, and responding to data, making them essential for the functionality of IoT applications.

1. **Sensors**
   - o **Definition:** Sensors are devices that detect physical properties (such as temperature, light, humidity, pressure, or motion) and convert these properties into digital data. Sensors are the eyes and ears of an IoT system, providing real-time environmental data.
   - o **Types of Sensors:**
     - ▪ **Temperature Sensors**: Measure temperature changes, often used in smart homes for thermostats or in industrial applications for equipment monitoring.
     - ▪ **Motion Sensors**: Detect movement in a given area and are commonly used in security systems.

26

- **Proximity Sensors**: Detect the presence of objects or people without physical contact, often found in automatic doors or retail inventory management.
- **Environmental Sensors**: Measure parameters like air quality, humidity, and pressure, used in weather stations, agriculture, and smart cities.
  - **Real-World Example:** Smart thermostats, such as Nest, use temperature sensors to monitor and adjust the room temperature based on real-time data, ensuring energy efficiency.

2. **Actuators**
   - **Definition:** Actuators are devices that receive commands from IoT systems and take action, usually by moving or controlling a mechanism. In simpler terms, actuators are responsible for executing physical actions based on the data received from sensors.
   - **Types of Actuators:**
     - **Electric Motors**: Convert electrical energy into mechanical motion, used in automated machinery or robotic systems.
     - **Hydraulic and Pneumatic Actuators**: Control the movement of machines in heavy industries by using fluid pressure.

27

- **Relays and Solenoids**: Used in switching applications, for example, to control the opening and closing of valves in a smart home water system.

o **Real-World Example:** In a smart home, an actuator can control the position of blinds or curtains. When the IoT system receives data about the current sunlight intensity, the actuator will open or close the blinds to maintain a set room temperature.

3. **Devices**

o **Definition:** Devices refer to the physical objects or equipment that make up the IoT ecosystem. They include sensors and actuators but also encompass the computing hardware that processes the data and communicates with other components of the system.

o **Types of Devices:**

- **Wearable Devices**: Examples include fitness trackers or smartwatches, which monitor activity, heart rate, and other health data.

- **Home Automation Devices**: Smart light bulbs, smart locks, and security cameras fall under this category, providing automated control and monitoring.

- **Industrial Devices**: In manufacturing, machines equipped with IoT devices allow for real-time monitoring and predictive maintenance.

Communication Protocols

IoT devices need to communicate with each other and with central systems, such as cloud servers. Communication protocols enable these interactions, ensuring devices can exchange data efficiently, securely, and reliably. These protocols define the rules for how data is transmitted between devices in an IoT network.

1. **Wi-Fi**
   - **Overview**: Wi-Fi is a common and widely used protocol for short-range communication, often found in consumer IoT applications like smart home devices.
   - **Strengths**: High-speed data transmission, ubiquitous coverage in homes and offices.
   - **Weaknesses**: Power consumption can be high, and it may not be suitable for low-power devices.

2. **Bluetooth**

- o **Overview**: Bluetooth is another widely used communication protocol for short-range communication, particularly in wearables and devices like fitness trackers or headphones.
- o **Strengths**: Low power consumption, good for personal area networks.
- o **Weaknesses**: Limited range (typically under 100 meters) and slower data transmission compared to Wi-Fi.

3. **Zigbee**

- o **Overview**: Zigbee is designed for low-power, low-data-rate applications. It's commonly used in home automation systems like smart lighting and heating.
- o **Strengths**: Low power consumption, supports mesh networking (devices can relay data to one another).
- o **Weaknesses**: Limited bandwidth and range.

4. **LoRaWAN (Long Range Wide Area Network)**

- o **Overview**: LoRaWAN is designed for long-range, low-power applications, making it ideal for remote IoT devices.
- o **Strengths**: Long-range communication (up to 10 kilometers), low power consumption.
- o **Weaknesses**: Low data transfer rates.

5. **Cellular Networks (LTE, 5G)**

- o **Overview**: Cellular networks like LTE and 5G are used in IoT applications that require wider coverage, such as in connected vehicles or remote monitoring systems.
- o **Strengths**: Wide coverage, reliable, supports high-speed data transfer.
- o **Weaknesses**: Higher cost for data transmission, especially for low-power devices.

6. **NB-IoT (Narrowband IoT)**

- o **Overview**: A cellular technology designed specifically for IoT applications that require low power and low bandwidth, such as smart meters or sensors.
- o **Strengths**: Low cost, low power, wide area coverage.
- o **Weaknesses**: Low data transfer rate, not suitable for high-speed applications.

7. **MQTT (Message Queuing Telemetry Transport)**

- o **Overview**: MQTT is a lightweight messaging protocol used for real-time communication in IoT systems.
- o **Strengths**: Minimal overhead, great for low-bandwidth, high-latency networks.
- o **Weaknesses**: Can be prone to data loss without proper message retention and QoS settings.

31

Cloud and Edge Computing

Both cloud and edge computing are essential to IoT architectures, providing the computational power and storage needed for processing the large amounts of data generated by IoT devices. However, they serve different roles in the IoT ecosystem.

1. **Cloud Computing**
   o **Definition**: Cloud computing refers to the delivery of computing services (such as storage, processing power, and databases) over the internet. In IoT, cloud platforms receive and store the massive data generated by devices and provide analytics and decision-making capabilities.
   o **Benefits:**
     ▪ Scalability: Cloud platforms can scale resources up or down based on demand, making them ideal for IoT systems with fluctuating data needs.
     ▪ Accessibility: Cloud platforms enable remote access to IoT data, allowing users to monitor and control devices from anywhere.

- Big Data Analytics: Cloud services offer powerful analytics tools, such as AI and machine learning, to process and analyze IoT data.

o **Real-World Example**: Amazon Web Services (AWS) and Microsoft Azure provide cloud-based IoT platforms that enable companies to connect, monitor, and analyze IoT devices remotely.

2. **Edge Computing**

o **Definition**: Edge computing involves processing data closer to the source of data generation, such as on IoT devices or local edge servers, rather than sending all data to the cloud. This approach reduces latency, lowers bandwidth usage, and enables real-time decision-making.

o **Benefits:**

- Reduced Latency: By processing data locally, edge computing enables real-time analytics and faster decision-making.

- Reduced Bandwidth Usage: Instead of sending all data to the cloud, only relevant information is transmitted, reducing data transfer costs.

- Enhanced Security: Data processed locally is less vulnerable to potential breaches during transmission.

  o **Real-World Example**: In autonomous vehicles, edge computing allows for real-time processing of sensor data (e.g., from cameras, radar, and LiDAR), enabling instant decisions, such as braking or steering adjustments.

This chapter introduces the essential components that form the backbone of any IoT system, providing the necessary infrastructure for data collection, communication, and processing. These components are critical for designing IoT solutions that are efficient, scalable, and responsive to real-time needs. Would you like to explore any specific component further or see more detailed examples?

CHAPTER 4

IOT ARCHITECTURE OVERVIEW

Layers of IoT Architecture

IoT architecture refers to the structure that defines how devices, networks, data processing, and applications interact within an IoT ecosystem. A typical IoT architecture is built on several layers that work together to ensure seamless communication, data processing, and real-time decision-making.

1. **Perception Layer (Sensing Layer)**
    o **Description:** The perception layer is responsible for the physical collection of data. It consists of the sensors, actuators, and devices that detect physical properties (temperature, humidity, motion, etc.) and convert them into digital signals.
    o **Components:** Sensors, RFID tags, cameras, and other sensing devices.
    o **Example:** A temperature sensor in a smart thermostat that collects data about room temperature.

2. **Network Layer (Transmission Layer)**

- o **Description:** This layer facilitates communication between the devices and the data storage or processing components of the system. It transmits the data collected by sensors to the processing system (either cloud or edge). The network layer is responsible for choosing the appropriate communication protocols (e.g., Wi-Fi, Bluetooth, Zigbee, etc.) and ensuring the integrity of the data during transmission.
- o **Components:** Routers, gateways, communication networks (e.g., Wi-Fi, cellular, LoRaWAN).
- o **Example:** A Wi-Fi network that connects a smart home device to the internet.

3. **Edge Layer (Processing Layer)**

- o **Description:** The edge layer processes the data closer to where it is generated (i.e., near the devices or on local servers). This minimizes latency and bandwidth usage by allowing real-time data analysis and decision-making without needing to send all data to the cloud.
- o **Components:** Edge devices, local servers, IoT gateways.
- o **Example:** A smart camera in a security system that processes video footage locally to detect

motion before sending relevant alerts to the cloud.

4. Data Processing Layer (Middleware)

- o **Description:** This layer manages and processes the data collected by IoT devices. It often acts as a bridge between the edge layer and the cloud. The data is cleaned, filtered, aggregated, and analyzed for further decision-making. This layer can involve middleware platforms or data analytics services.

- o **Components:** Data aggregation tools, data transformation systems, middleware platforms.

- o **Example:** A cloud platform that receives data from various IoT devices, aggregates the data, and transforms it into a usable format for analysis.

5. Application Layer

- o **Description:** This layer consists of the software applications and interfaces that enable users to interact with IoT systems. It allows for visualizing data, controlling devices, and taking actions based on insights. This layer is where the end-users benefit from IoT functionalities.

- o **Components:** IoT dashboards, mobile apps, control interfaces.

- o **Example:** A mobile app that allows users to remotely control home lighting and temperature.

6. **Business Layer**

- o **Description:** The business layer involves the management of the IoT system's overall functionality and strategy. This layer focuses on the business logic, goals, and user experience, ensuring that the IoT system meets the needs of the business or end-users.

- o **Components:** Business management systems, IoT system strategies, business analytics.

- o **Example:** A company using IoT data to drive decisions about supply chain optimization.

IoT Systems: Edge, Gateway, and Cloud

IoT systems are often comprised of three major components: edge, gateway, and cloud, each playing a unique role in the processing and transmission of data.

1. **Edge Computing**

- o **Description:** Edge computing refers to processing data at the source (close to the IoT devices) rather than sending it to a centralized data center or cloud. Edge computing enables faster decision-making, reduces bandwidth usage, and enhances privacy.

- o **Role in IoT:** Edge devices process sensor data locally and only send necessary or summarized data to the cloud or central server.
- o **Example:** In industrial IoT, sensors on factory machines detect anomalies like vibration or temperature, and edge computing devices analyze this data locally to trigger real-time maintenance alerts.

2. Gateway

- o **Description:** The gateway acts as a bridge between the IoT devices (sensors and actuators) and the cloud or edge processing systems. It collects data from multiple devices, preprocesses it, and sends it over the network to the cloud or edge computing platform.
- o **Role in IoT:** The gateway facilitates communication between various devices using different communication protocols and the cloud or edge server, ensuring data consistency and security.
- o **Example:** In a smart factory, a gateway aggregates data from sensors on multiple machines and sends it to the cloud platform for further analysis and reporting.

3. Cloud Computing

o **Description:** Cloud computing involves the storage, management, and processing of IoT data in remote, centralized servers that can be accessed over the internet. The cloud allows for scalable data storage and advanced analytics, supporting large-scale IoT deployments.

o **Role in IoT:** The cloud handles large-scale data processing and analytics. It stores vast amounts of data collected from IoT devices and provides services like real-time data analysis, machine learning, and application hosting.

o **Example:** A smart city uses cloud-based platforms to monitor traffic patterns, collect data from thousands of IoT sensors, and analyze the data to optimize traffic flow in real-time.

Real-World Use Cases

Here are several real-world use cases that illustrate how IoT architecture is applied across different industries:

1. **Smart Homes**

   o **IoT Components:** Sensors (motion, temperature), devices (smart thermostats, security cameras), cloud platforms.

40

- o **Use Case**: In a smart home, motion sensors and smart cameras detect movement and transmit this data to the cloud, where it is analyzed. If an intruder is detected, a real-time alert is sent to the homeowner via a mobile app.
- o **IoT Architecture**: Sensors collect data (Perception Layer), the data is sent via Wi-Fi (Network Layer) to a cloud platform for analysis (Cloud), and the homeowner receives a notification through an app (Application Layer).

2. Industrial IoT (IIoT)

- o **IoT Components**: Sensors (temperature, pressure), actuators, gateways, edge computing devices.
- o **Use Case**: In manufacturing, IIoT devices monitor machine performance in real-time. Data is processed on edge devices for immediate decisions (e.g., stopping a machine to prevent failure), and relevant data is sent to the cloud for long-term analytics.
- o **IoT Architecture**: Sensors collect data (Perception Layer), edge computing devices process data (Edge Layer), the gateway aggregates and sends it to the cloud (Network Layer), and the analysis is used to predict

maintenance needs (Cloud/Data Processing Layer).

3. **Smart Cities**

   o **IoT Components**: Environmental sensors (air quality, temperature), communication networks, cloud platforms, data analytics tools.

   o **Use Case**: In a smart city, IoT sensors are placed around urban areas to monitor air quality, weather conditions, and traffic patterns. Data is processed on edge devices and sent to the cloud for further analysis, where city planners can optimize infrastructure based on real-time data.

   o **IoT Architecture**: Sensors collect environmental data (Perception Layer), data is transmitted through a wireless network (Network Layer), analyzed in the cloud (Cloud), and used for urban planning decisions (Application Layer).

4. **Healthcare IoT**

   o **IoT Components**: Wearable devices (heart rate monitors, glucose meters), cloud computing, mobile apps.

   o **Use Case**: Wearable devices collect patient health data in real-time and transmit it to the cloud for storage and analysis. Healthcare providers can access the data through

42

applications and make informed decisions about patient care.

o **IoT Architecture**: Wearables collect data (Perception Layer), data is transmitted via a wireless network (Network Layer), processed and stored in the cloud (Cloud), and made available to doctors via an app (Application Layer).

This chapter outlines the key components of IoT architecture and how they work together to deliver value through efficient, real-time data collection, processing, and decision-making. Whether it's at the edge, in the cloud, or through a gateway, each layer plays an important role in making IoT systems effective and scalable.

CHAPTER 5

COMMUNICATION PROTOCOLS IN IOT

Bluetooth, Wi-Fi, Zigbee, LoRaWAN, and More

Communication protocols are the backbone of any IoT system, as they enable devices to send and receive data efficiently and securely. The choice of protocol affects an IoT solution's performance, scalability, and energy efficiency. Here's an overview of some of the most commonly used communication protocols in IoT:

1. **Bluetooth**
    - o **Overview:** Bluetooth is a short-range wireless communication protocol that is commonly used for personal area networks (PANs). It operates in the 2.4 GHz ISM (Industrial, Scientific, and Medical) band and is optimized for low-power applications.
    - o **Strengths:**
        - ▪ Low energy consumption (especially with Bluetooth Low Energy or BLE).

44

- Ideal for applications like wearables, fitness trackers, and smart home devices.
- Supported by most mobile devices, making it great for consumer IoT applications.

o **Weaknesses:**

- Limited range (typically up to 100 meters).
- Slower data transfer rates compared to other protocols like Wi-Fi.

o **Real-World Example:** Bluetooth is commonly used in fitness devices like smartwatches (e.g., Apple Watch or Fitbit), where data is transmitted from the device to the user's smartphone.

2. **Wi-Fi**

o **Overview:** Wi-Fi is one of the most widely used wireless communication protocols, offering high-speed internet connectivity. It operates in the 2.4 GHz and 5 GHz bands and is ideal for applications requiring larger amounts of data and internet connectivity.

o **Strengths:**

- High data transfer rates, which makes it suitable for data-heavy applications.

45

- Widely available infrastructure in homes, offices, and public spaces.
- Supports long-range communication (up to several hundred meters).

o **Weaknesses:**

- Higher power consumption, making it less suitable for battery-operated devices.
- Limited scalability for large networks compared to protocols like Zigbee.

o **Real-World Example:** Smart home devices like Nest thermostats and smart cameras use Wi-Fi to connect to the internet and allow users to control their devices remotely.

3. **Zigbee**

o **Overview:** Zigbee is a low-power, low-data-rate wireless communication protocol, designed specifically for IoT devices in home automation, industrial, and smart city applications. It operates in the 2.4 GHz, 868 MHz, and 915 MHz frequency bands.

o **Strengths:**

- Low power consumption, making it ideal for battery-operated devices.

- Mesh networking capability, which allows devices to communicate with each other and extend the network range.
- Ideal for small data transmissions, such as sensor data.

o **Weaknesses:**
  - Lower data transfer rates compared to Wi-Fi and Bluetooth.
  - Limited range (up to 100 meters), though the mesh network can help expand coverage.

o **Real-World Example:** Zigbee is widely used in smart home automation systems, such as Philips Hue smart lights, which use Zigbee to enable communication between lights, sensors, and the control hub.

4. **LoRaWAN (Long Range Wide Area Network)**
   o **Overview:** LoRaWAN is a protocol designed for long-range, low-power communication in IoT applications that need to cover large areas, such as agricultural and environmental monitoring.
   o **Strengths:**
     - Long-range communication (up to 10 kilometers in rural areas).

- Extremely low power consumption, enabling devices to last for years on a single battery.
- Supports large-scale IoT deployments due to its ability to connect thousands of devices over wide areas.

o **Weaknesses:**

- Low data rates, making it unsuitable for applications that require large amounts of data.
- Requires dedicated gateways to facilitate communication between devices and the network.

o **Real-World Example:** LoRaWAN is commonly used in agriculture to monitor soil moisture, temperature, and other environmental factors across large farms or rural areas.

5. **NFC (Near Field Communication)**

o **Overview:** NFC is a short-range wireless communication protocol that allows devices to communicate when they are within close proximity, typically within 4 cm.

o **Strengths:**

- Secure and simple communication, often used for payment systems.
- Low power consumption, as devices only activate when they are in range.

- o **Weaknesses:**
  - Very short communication range, which limits its use in larger IoT networks.
  - Limited data transfer rate.
- o **Real-World Example:** NFC is widely used in contactless payment systems like Apple Pay or Google Pay, where smartphones or smart cards communicate with point-of-sale terminals.

6. **Cellular Networks (2G, 3G, 4G, 5G)**
   - o **Overview:** Cellular networks provide wide-area coverage using cellular infrastructure. With the rollout of 5G, the potential for IoT applications requiring high bandwidth, low latency, and high reliability has increased.
   - o **Strengths:**
     - Extensive coverage, especially in urban areas.
     - Reliable and secure communication, making it suitable for applications like connected vehicles or asset tracking.

49

- 5G offers ultra-low latency and faster speeds for real-time applications.
  - **Weaknesses:**
    - Higher data costs compared to other IoT protocols like LoRaWAN.
    - Limited availability of 5G in rural or remote areas.
  - **Real-World Example:** Connected vehicles use cellular networks to transmit real-time data about their location, speed, and condition to the cloud for analysis.

How Protocols Impact IoT Applications

The choice of communication protocol has a significant impact on how an IoT system performs, operates, and scales. Each protocol offers distinct advantages and trade-offs that must be considered based on the application's specific requirements. Here's how the protocols can affect different aspects of IoT applications:

1. **Power Consumption**
   - Protocols like **Bluetooth Low Energy (BLE)**, **Zigbee**, and **LoRaWAN** are designed for low-power devices, which is essential for battery-

operated IoT applications. Devices that rely on these protocols can operate for years without needing a battery change.

- o **Wi-Fi** and **cellular networks** consume more power, which makes them less suitable for devices that need to run on limited battery power for extended periods.

2. Data Transfer Rates

- o **Wi-Fi** and **cellular networks** (especially 5G) are ideal for applications that need to transmit large amounts of data quickly, such as video streaming or large file transfers.
- o **Zigbee**, **LoRaWAN**, and **Bluetooth** are better suited for low-data-rate applications, like sensor data collection or simple commands.

3. Range

- o If long-range communication is necessary, protocols like **LoRaWAN** or **cellular networks** are the best choices, with ranges of several kilometers.
- o For short-range communication, **Bluetooth** and **NFC** work well, but their range is limited to a few meters.

4. Network Topology

- o **Zigbee** supports mesh networking, where devices can relay data to each other, expanding the

51

network range. This is ideal for applications in home automation or smart cities, where many devices need to communicate over a large area.

o **Wi-Fi** operates in a star topology, with devices communicating through a central access point, while **LoRaWAN** works in a star network with gateways serving as the central communication point.

Choosing the Right Protocol for Different Applications

When designing an IoT solution, it's crucial to select the right communication protocol based on the specific needs of the application. Here are some guidelines to help choose the right protocol:

1. **For Smart Home Devices**:

   o **Best Choice**: **Wi-Fi** or **Zigbee**

   o **Why?** Wi-Fi provides high-speed internet connectivity for devices like smart cameras, thermostats, and lights. **Zigbee** is ideal for low-power devices in home automation systems.

2. **For Wearables and Personal Devices**:

   o **Best Choice**: **Bluetooth Low Energy (BLE)**

52

- o **Why?** BLE offers low power consumption and is widely used in fitness trackers, smartwatches, and health-monitoring devices, where battery life is critical.

3. **For Industrial IoT and Asset Tracking**:
   - o **Best Choice**: **LoRaWAN** or **Cellular Networks**
   - o **Why?** LoRaWAN is ideal for large-scale deployments in rural or remote locations, while **cellular networks** (especially 5G) provide reliable connectivity for real-time industrial applications.

4. **For Payment Systems**:
   - o **Best Choice**: **NFC**
   - o **Why?** NFC is designed for very short-range communication, making it perfect for secure, contactless payments.

This chapter provides an in-depth look at communication protocols and how they influence the performance and functionality of IoT applications. By understanding the strengths and weaknesses of each protocol, you can choose the one that best fits your IoT solution's needs.

CHAPTER 6

IOT DEVICES AND SENSORS

Types of IoT Devices: Wearables, Smart Home Devices, Industrial Sensors

IoT devices come in various forms, and their applications span across different industries, from healthcare and home automation to manufacturing and agriculture. Here's a look at the most common types of IoT devices:

1. **Wearable Devices**
   - o **Description:** Wearables are small electronic devices that can be worn on the body, such as smartwatches, fitness trackers, and health-monitoring devices. These devices are typically embedded with sensors that track various health parameters and activity metrics.
   - o **Examples:**
     - **Smartwatches** like the Apple Watch or Samsung Galaxy Watch monitor heart rate, track physical activity, and provide notifications.

- **Fitness trackers** such as Fitbit or Xiaomi Mi Band track steps, calories burned, and sleep patterns.
- **Health monitoring devices** like smart rings (e.g., Oura Ring) that track body temperature, sleep quality, and other vital signs.

o **Use Cases:** Wearables are commonly used for fitness and health monitoring, providing real-time feedback to users. They also help track vital signs and health conditions, making them valuable tools for preventive healthcare.

2. **Smart Home Devices**

o **Description:** Smart home devices enhance convenience, security, and energy efficiency in the home. They are typically connected to a central hub or app that allows users to control and monitor them remotely.

o **Examples:**

- **Smart thermostats** like the Nest Thermostat, which learns the user's temperature preferences and adjusts the heating and cooling accordingly.
- **Smart lighting systems** like Philips Hue, which allow users to adjust lighting remotely or set automated schedules.

- **Smart locks** that enable keyless entry and remote locking/unlocking through a smartphone app.
- **Smart security cameras** like Ring or Arlo, which provide real-time video surveillance and can send alerts to users' smartphones.

o **Use Cases:** These devices provide enhanced comfort, energy management, and security. For instance, smart thermostats optimize energy use by adjusting temperatures based on occupancy, and smart locks offer remote access control for homes.

3. **Industrial Sensors**

o **Description:** Industrial IoT (IIoT) sensors are designed to monitor and improve the performance of machinery and equipment in various industries, such as manufacturing, logistics, and energy.

o **Examples:**

- **Temperature sensors** that monitor machine heat levels to prevent overheating.
- **Vibration sensors** used in predictive maintenance to detect early signs of mechanical failure.

56

- **Pressure sensors** that track fluid levels in tanks and pipes, ensuring optimal performance in industrial settings.
- **Proximity sensors** that detect the presence of objects or people, commonly used in automated factories.

  o **Use Cases:** Industrial sensors are used for predictive maintenance, quality control, process optimization, and resource monitoring. For example, temperature and vibration sensors help prevent machine breakdowns by alerting operators when maintenance is needed.

How Sensors Collect Data

Sensors are the primary components in IoT systems responsible for collecting real-time data. The way sensors collect data depends on the type of sensor and the physical properties they are designed to measure. Here's a closer look at how sensors gather information:

1. **Detection of Physical Changes**
   o Sensors detect physical changes in the environment, such as temperature, pressure, motion, or light. These changes are converted

into electrical signals that can be transmitted to other devices or systems for further analysis.

o **Example:** A temperature sensor detects the heat in the environment. When the temperature rises or falls, the sensor converts this change into an electrical signal that is sent to a controller or cloud system.

2. **Analog to Digital Conversion**

o Many sensors produce analog signals (continuous signals), but IoT systems typically work with digital signals (discrete values). Therefore, the sensor's output often needs to be converted into a digital format using an **Analog-to-Digital Converter (ADC)** before it can be processed by microcontrollers or transmitted over networks.

o **Example:** A light sensor may measure the intensity of light in an environment, providing a continuous voltage. This signal is then converted into a digital value for use in applications like adjusting the brightness of smart lighting systems.

3. **Wireless Transmission of Data**

o Once data is collected, sensors transmit it to other devices or systems. In IoT, this data is often transmitted wirelessly via communication protocols such as Wi-Fi, Bluetooth, Zigbee, or LoRaWAN.

- o **Example:** A motion sensor in a smart home system detects movement and sends a signal to the connected smart security camera, which can then trigger an alert or start recording.

4. **Real-Time Data Streaming**

- o Many IoT sensors are designed to provide real-time data, enabling immediate action. For instance, wearables continuously monitor heart rate or steps, while industrial sensors track machine performance in real-time to prevent failures.

- o **Example:** A GPS sensor on a vehicle transmits its location data to a fleet management system, enabling real-time tracking and optimization of delivery routes.

Applications of IoT Sensors in Daily Life

IoT sensors are embedded in everyday objects, providing valuable insights and making life more convenient, efficient, and secure. Here are some examples of how sensors are used in daily life:

1. **Health and Fitness Monitoring**

- o **Wearable Sensors:** Fitness trackers and smartwatches equipped with sensors monitor vital signs like heart rate, oxygen levels, and activity levels. This data is used to track fitness progress, provide health insights, and offer personalized recommendations.
- o **Example:** A fitness tracker like Fitbit uses sensors to monitor your daily steps and heart rate. It then sends the data to a smartphone app, where users can track their progress over time.

2. **Smart Home Automation**

- o **Environmental Sensors:** Sensors in smart home devices monitor various environmental factors such as temperature, humidity, and light. These sensors help optimize comfort, energy usage, and security in homes.
- o **Example:** A smart thermostat uses temperature sensors to adjust the heating and cooling system based on your preferences or the time of day, helping to save energy and keep your home comfortable.

3. **Security and Surveillance**

- o **Motion and Proximity Sensors:** These sensors are crucial in smart security systems, helping detect unauthorized movements or activities.

Security cameras, smart locks, and alarm systems rely on these sensors for real-time surveillance.

o **Example:** Smart cameras like Ring use motion sensors to detect movement around your property and send real-time alerts to your phone. These systems can also trigger video recording or alert the police if necessary.

4. Environmental Monitoring

o **Air Quality Sensors:** In urban areas, air quality sensors are used to monitor pollutants and provide real-time air quality reports to citizens. These sensors help identify pollution levels, which can lead to better public health measures.

o **Example:** Air quality sensors in smart cities monitor pollutants like carbon dioxide (CO_2) and particulate matter (PM). This data helps local governments issue alerts to residents and take actions to reduce pollution levels.

5. Energy Management

o **Smart Meters and Energy Sensors:** These sensors monitor energy consumption and help reduce waste by enabling users to manage their electricity usage more efficiently.

o **Example:** Smart meters in homes track energy usage in real-time and provide detailed reports to homeowners, enabling them to adjust their consumption habits to save on energy bills.

6. **Agriculture and Farming**

   o **Soil and Environmental Sensors:** In agriculture, IoT sensors are used to monitor soil conditions, moisture levels, and environmental factors like temperature. This data helps farmers optimize irrigation and crop management practices, improving yields.

   o **Example:** Smart irrigation systems use soil moisture sensors to determine when and how much water to apply to crops, ensuring efficient water use and healthy crop growth.

This chapter introduces the types of IoT devices and sensors, explaining how they collect data and their numerous applications in daily life. From health monitoring to energy management, IoT sensors are becoming an integral part of making everyday activities smarter, more efficient, and more convenient.

CHAPTER 7

DATA MANAGEMENT IN IOT

The Role of Data in IoT

Data is the core of the Internet of Things (IoT). IoT devices and sensors generate massive amounts of data by continuously monitoring and collecting information from the physical world. This data is used to derive insights, make real-time decisions, and enable automation. The role of data in IoT can be summarized in three key areas:

1. **Real-Time Decision Making**
   - o IoT systems are designed to respond to changing conditions in real time. For instance, a smart thermostat uses data from temperature sensors to adjust the heating or cooling of a room instantly. Similarly, in industrial IoT (IIoT), sensors on machinery provide continuous data to predict failures before they occur, allowing for timely maintenance.
   - o **Example:** In autonomous vehicles, data from cameras, radar, and LiDAR sensors is processed in real-time to make driving decisions, such as

adjusting speed or steering based on road conditions or obstacles.

2. Predictive Analytics and Optimization

o IoT data can be analyzed to identify trends, patterns, and correlations, which help improve efficiency and predict future events. Predictive analytics can optimize system performance, reduce downtime, and enable proactive decision-making. This is especially valuable in sectors like manufacturing, healthcare, and energy.

o **Example:** In healthcare, continuous monitoring data from wearable devices can predict potential health issues, like an impending heart attack, allowing for early intervention.

3. Automation and Process Control

o One of the major benefits of IoT is automation. With real-time data, IoT systems can make autonomous decisions to control devices, systems, or processes without human intervention. This is essential for industries that require constant monitoring and fast response times, like energy management, transportation, and agriculture.

o **Example:** In smart agriculture, IoT sensors monitor soil moisture levels and automatically adjust irrigation systems, ensuring crops receive the right amount of water at the right time.

Data Collection, Storage, and Analysis

The process of managing data in an IoT system involves three primary steps: collection, storage, and analysis. These steps enable the transformation of raw data into actionable insights.

1. **Data Collection**
   o **How Data is Collected:** IoT devices collect data through various sensors that measure physical properties like temperature, pressure, motion, and humidity. Data collection happens continuously or at set intervals, depending on the application and sensor type.
   o **Data Formats:** IoT devices often produce different types of data, including numeric values (e.g., temperature readings), categorical values (e.g., on/off states of a device), and complex data (e.g., video footage from security cameras).
   o **Challenges:** Data collection in IoT systems can be overwhelming due to the sheer volume of data being generated. Filtering and preprocessing the

data before transmission to ensure its relevance is crucial for efficiency.

2. **Data Storage**

   o **How Data is Stored:** Once data is collected, it needs to be stored for further processing and analysis. Storage can occur locally (on the device itself or an edge computing device) or in the cloud.

   o **Types of Data Storage:**

     ▪ **Edge Storage:** In edge computing, some data is stored on local devices or edge servers. This is useful for applications that require real-time processing and minimal latency, such as autonomous vehicles or industrial machinery.

     ▪ **Cloud Storage:** For most IoT applications, data is stored in cloud platforms. Cloud storage allows for scalable, centralized storage and access, enabling data to be analyzed, shared, and archived across devices and locations.

   o **Challenges:** The volume of data generated by IoT devices is enormous, which presents challenges related to storage capacity, data redundancy, and data security. Managing this

66

data efficiently is key to ensuring the long-term viability of IoT systems.

3. **Data Analysis**

o **Purpose of Data Analysis:** Data analysis involves processing collected data to extract meaningful insights, identify patterns, and inform decision-making. IoT systems typically perform two types of data analysis:

- **Real-Time Analysis:** In real-time systems, data is analyzed as it's generated, enabling immediate responses. This is vital in applications like smart home systems, where the thermostat needs to adjust instantly when temperature readings change.

- **Batch Analysis:** In many cases, IoT data is stored and analyzed in batches, allowing for deeper analysis over time. This is common in industrial settings where historical data is analyzed to predict equipment failures or optimize production schedules.

o **Tools for Analysis:** IoT data analysis often involves big data tools and platforms like **Apache Hadoop**, **Apache Spark**, and cloud-based analytics platforms such as **Google Cloud IoT** or **AWS IoT Analytics**.

Cloud vs. On-Premise Data Storage

The choice of data storage solution—cloud or on-premise—depends on various factors, such as the volume of data, security requirements, latency concerns, and cost considerations. Let's explore both options:

1. **Cloud Data Storage**
   - **Description:** Cloud storage refers to storing data in remote servers managed by third-party service providers (e.g., AWS, Microsoft Azure, Google Cloud). The cloud offers vast storage capacity and provides access to powerful analytics tools, making it an attractive option for IoT applications that require centralized data processing.
   - **Advantages:**
     - **Scalability:** Cloud platforms provide on-demand storage, making it easy to scale up or down based on IoT system needs.
     - **Remote Access:** Data stored in the cloud can be accessed from anywhere, enabling

remote monitoring and management of IoT devices.

- **Advanced Analytics:** Cloud platforms offer advanced analytics and machine learning tools that can help derive insights from large datasets.
- **Reduced Infrastructure Costs:** There's no need for on-site hardware or maintenance, as cloud providers handle the infrastructure.

o **Disadvantages:**

- **Latency:** Depending on the application, cloud storage may introduce latency, which can be problematic for real-time systems.
- **Security Concerns:** Data stored in the cloud is at risk of breaches or unauthorized access if not properly secured.
- **Ongoing Costs:** While cloud storage eliminates the need for physical infrastructure, ongoing operational costs (e.g., data transfer fees) can add up over time.

o **Example:** Smart cities often use cloud storage to store and analyze data from thousands of IoT sensors, such as traffic cameras, air quality monitors, and smart street lights.

2. **On-Premise Data Storage**

o **Description:** On-premise storage involves storing data locally on physical servers within an organization's infrastructure. It's typically used in IoT systems that require high security, low latency, or where data sovereignty laws mandate local storage.

o **Advantages:**

▪ **Low Latency:** On-premise storage allows for faster data access and real-time processing, as the data is stored close to the IoT devices.

▪ **Full Control:** Organizations have complete control over their data and infrastructure, which is critical for industries with strict security or regulatory requirements.

▪ **Security:** On-premise storage allows organizations to implement their own security measures and policies.

o **Disadvantages:**

- **Limited Scalability:** On-premise storage can be expensive and less flexible than cloud storage, as organizations need to manage physical hardware and expand infrastructure as data grows.
- **High Maintenance Costs:** Maintaining on-premise servers requires dedicated IT resources, which can be costly and time-consuming.
- **Geographic Limitations:** On-premise storage is typically accessible only within the organization's local network, limiting remote access to data.

o **Example:** Critical infrastructure systems, like power plants or healthcare facilities, often use on-premise data storage to ensure low-latency access to operational data and comply with data security standards.

This chapter provides an overview of data management in IoT, detailing how data is collected, stored, and analyzed to extract valuable insights. The decision between cloud and on-premise storage is a key consideration for IoT implementations, depending on the application's specific

71

CHAPTER 8

CLOUD COMPUTING AND IOT

How Cloud Platforms Support IoT Applications

Cloud computing has become a critical component of many IoT applications. The cloud offers a scalable, flexible, and cost-effective solution for managing the vast amounts of data generated by IoT devices. Here's how cloud platforms support IoT applications:

1. **Data Storage and Management**
   - o IoT devices generate vast amounts of data, and the cloud provides a centralized place to store this data. Cloud platforms offer virtually unlimited storage capacity, ensuring that data from thousands (or even millions) of IoT devices can be stored and accessed as needed. The cloud can handle structured and unstructured data, which is essential for processing the diverse types of data IoT devices generate.
   - o **Example:** Data from sensors monitoring the temperature, humidity, and air quality in a smart city can be stored in the cloud for analysis,

making it easy to scale as the number of connected devices increases.

2. Data Processing and Analytics

- o Cloud platforms provide the necessary computational resources for processing and analyzing the large volumes of IoT data. IoT data often needs to be processed in real-time (for immediate action) or in batch mode (for deeper analysis), and the cloud enables both.

- o **Example:** In a smart manufacturing plant, cloud computing enables the real-time analysis of sensor data from machines. It can help detect anomalies like temperature spikes or vibration, allowing for predictive maintenance and reducing downtime.

3. Connectivity and Scalability

- o Cloud platforms offer seamless connectivity between IoT devices and the applications that process their data. With the cloud, new devices can be easily added to the system without the need for complex infrastructure changes. This scalability is crucial for growing IoT ecosystems.

- o **Example:** A smart home system can easily integrate new devices, such as smart bulbs or security cameras, into the cloud infrastructure, allowing users to control and monitor these devices from anywhere.

4. **Edge and Cloud Integration**

o While the cloud is essential for large-scale storage and analytics, edge computing complements it by processing data closer to the source (i.e., on IoT devices or local servers). Many cloud platforms support hybrid architectures that combine both edge and cloud computing to ensure low-latency decision-making while still benefiting from cloud-based scalability.

o **Example:** In autonomous vehicles, cloud computing is used to store and analyze historical data, while edge computing processes sensor data in real-time for driving decisions like braking or navigation.

5. **Security and Privacy**

o Security is a major concern for IoT systems, as sensitive data can be vulnerable to attacks. Cloud platforms offer robust security features, including data encryption, secure communication protocols, and identity management, to ensure the safety of IoT data.

o **Example:** A healthcare application that collects patient data from wearable devices uses cloud-based encryption and secure communication channels to ensure patient privacy and compliance with regulations like HIPAA (Health Insurance Portability and Accountability Act).

Key Cloud Providers and Services

Several major cloud providers offer IoT-specific services that enable businesses to build, deploy, and manage IoT applications efficiently. Here are some of the key cloud providers and the services they offer:

1. **Amazon Web Services (AWS)**
   o **IoT Core:** AWS IoT Core is a fully managed cloud service that allows IoT devices to securely connect and interact with cloud applications. It supports data processing, storage, and analysis of IoT data.
   o **AWS Lambda:** AWS Lambda enables serverless computing, allowing developers to run code in response to IoT events without managing servers. This service is ideal for real-time processing of IoT data.
   o **AWS IoT Analytics:** AWS IoT Analytics allows businesses to analyze large volumes of IoT data

and derive actionable insights. It includes data cleaning, processing, and visualization tools.

2. **Microsoft Azure**

   o **Azure IoT Hub:** Azure IoT Hub is a cloud service that facilitates the connection, monitoring, and management of IoT devices at scale. It supports bi-directional communication between devices and cloud applications.

   o **Azure IoT Central:** A fully managed IoT app platform that allows businesses to quickly deploy and manage IoT solutions without needing to write custom code. It's designed for both small and large IoT projects.

   o **Azure Digital Twins:** Azure Digital Twins is a platform that allows businesses to create digital replicas of physical environments, such as factories, buildings, or smart cities, for real-time monitoring and decision-making.

3. **Google Cloud**

   o **Google Cloud IoT Core:** Google Cloud IoT Core is a fully managed service that allows IoT devices to securely connect and transmit data to Google Cloud for analysis. It integrates well with Google's other services, such as BigQuery and Google Machine Learning tools.

o **Cloud Pub/Sub:** Google Cloud Pub/Sub is a messaging service that enables real-time data streaming and processing from IoT devices to cloud applications.

o **Google Cloud AI and ML Services:** Google Cloud offers powerful machine learning tools that can be used to analyze and predict trends from IoT data, helping businesses make data-driven decisions.

4. **IBM Cloud**

o **IBM Watson IoT Platform:** IBM Watson IoT Platform enables the connection of devices to the cloud and the collection, analysis, and management of IoT data. It integrates with Watson AI to provide insights and predictive analytics.

o **IBM Edge Application Manager:** A solution for managing and deploying edge devices and applications that are part of the IoT ecosystem, providing secure, automated device management.

o **IBM Cloud Pak for Data:** This platform provides data integration, governance, and analysis tools, supporting IoT data analysis and business intelligence.

5. **Oracle Cloud**

- o **Oracle IoT Cloud:** Oracle IoT Cloud offers solutions for managing and analyzing IoT data, including device connectivity, data storage, and predictive analytics.
- o **Oracle Autonomous Database:** This service automates the management of large-scale databases, allowing businesses to store and analyze vast amounts of IoT data efficiently.
- o **Oracle Cloud Infrastructure (OCI):** OCI provides high-performance computing resources that can be used to process and store IoT data, making it a suitable option for demanding IoT applications.

Real-World IoT Cloud Architecture Examples

The architecture of an IoT cloud system typically includes several key components: IoT devices, gateways, cloud storage, data processing tools, and applications. Below are some examples of real-world IoT cloud architectures:

1. **Smart Home System**
   - o **IoT Devices:** Smart thermostats, lighting systems, security cameras, and sensors.

- o **Gateway:** A hub or gateway connects the IoT devices to the cloud, enabling communication between devices and cloud services.
- o **Cloud Services:** The cloud platform manages data storage, device management, and user interaction. For instance, AWS IoT Core can connect devices securely to the cloud.
- o **Data Processing:** Data from devices is processed in the cloud using tools like AWS Lambda or Azure IoT Hub. Machine learning algorithms can analyze the data to predict user preferences and automate actions (e.g., adjusting room temperature).
- o **Applications:** Users interact with the system through mobile apps, which allow them to control devices remotely and receive real-time notifications.

2. **Industrial IoT (IIoT) in Manufacturing**

- o **IoT Devices:** Sensors monitor machine performance, temperature, humidity, vibration, and other critical factors on factory floors.
- o **Gateway:** IoT gateways collect data from sensors and transmit it to the cloud for analysis. Gateways can also perform some local processing to reduce the volume of data sent to the cloud.

- o **Cloud Services:** Cloud platforms like Microsoft Azure IoT Hub or AWS IoT Analytics handle the storage, processing, and analysis of the collected data.
- o **Data Processing:** Data is analyzed in real-time to identify anomalies (such as equipment wear) and trigger predictive maintenance alerts. Historical data is analyzed using cloud-based tools to optimize production schedules.
- o **Applications:** Factory managers receive dashboards and reports on equipment health, operational performance, and production efficiency. Alerts and recommendations are sent to mobile devices or email.

3. **Agriculture and Smart Farming**

- o **IoT Devices:** Soil moisture sensors, weather stations, temperature sensors, and automated irrigation systems.
- o **Gateway:** Gateways collect and aggregate data from field sensors, transmitting it to the cloud for analysis.
- o **Cloud Services:** Google Cloud IoT Core or AWS IoT can store and process the large volumes of data generated by agricultural sensors.

o **Data Processing:** The cloud performs analytics on weather data, soil conditions, and crop health to optimize irrigation schedules and fertilizer use.

o **Applications:** Farmers use mobile apps or web dashboards to monitor soil conditions, receive alerts about potential problems (like droughts), and manage irrigation and fertilization in real-time.

Cloud computing is a crucial enabler of IoT, providing the infrastructure for scalable, flexible, and efficient management of IoT data. Cloud platforms offer the storage, processing power, and analytics tools needed to make IoT applications smarter and more responsive.

CHAPTER 9

EDGE AND FOG COMPUTING

Defining Edge and Fog Computing

In the world of IoT, two computing paradigms, **edge computing** and **fog computing**, have emerged to address the challenges of processing data closer to where it is generated. These concepts are essential for managing the vast amounts of data generated by IoT devices, ensuring that processing can occur in real-time and with minimal latency.

1. **Edge Computing**
   o **Definition:** Edge computing refers to the practice of processing data at or near the source of data generation, which could be IoT devices or local servers. Instead of sending all data to a centralized cloud server for processing, edge computing enables local processing, reducing latency and bandwidth use.
   o **Example:** In a smart factory, sensors on machines gather real-time data about machine performance, which is then processed on-site (at the edge) to determine if maintenance is required or if an issue needs immediate attention.

2. **Fog Computing**

   o **Definition:** Fog computing, often used interchangeably with edge computing, involves a more distributed approach, where data processing happens on a local network of devices, which could be gateways, routers, or local servers. The term "fog" suggests a layer between the edge (local devices) and the cloud, creating a more distributed computing infrastructure that supports real-time decision-making.

   o **Example:** In a smart city, fog computing devices might aggregate data from traffic sensors, street lights, and surveillance cameras at the local level before sending it to the cloud for further analysis.

In both paradigms, data is processed closer to the source rather than relying solely on distant cloud data centers. This shift significantly improves real-time processing capabilities and reduces dependency on cloud infrastructure.

Benefits and Challenges of Edge Computing

Edge computing is gaining prominence due to its ability to process data locally, which leads to numerous benefits. However, it also comes with its own set of challenges.

Benefits:

1. **Reduced Latency**
   - **Explanation:** Since data processing occurs closer to the source (on the edge), edge computing reduces the time it takes for data to travel to distant cloud servers and back. This is especially important for applications requiring real-time decision-making, such as autonomous vehicles or industrial automation.
   - **Example:** In autonomous vehicles, real-time data from sensors like cameras and LIDAR needs to be processed almost instantly to make decisions about braking, steering, or acceleration. Edge computing ensures low-latency processing.

2. **Bandwidth Efficiency**
   - **Explanation:** With edge computing, only relevant or pre-processed data is sent to the cloud, reducing the amount of data transmitted over the network. This is especially useful for systems that generate vast amounts of data, like video surveillance or IoT sensors.
   - **Example:** A smart factory uses local edge devices to process sensor data and only sends critical information (e.g., alerts about machine

failure) to the cloud, reducing network congestion and costs.

3. **Improved Security and Privacy**

   o **Explanation:** By keeping data local and processing it on-site, sensitive information doesn't have to be sent across the internet, reducing the risk of data breaches or cyberattacks. This is particularly important in industries with strict data privacy regulations, such as healthcare and finance.

   o **Example:** In healthcare, edge computing can process patient data from wearable devices on-site at a hospital, ensuring that sensitive health data isn't transmitted to the cloud unless necessary for long-term storage or analysis.

4. **Reliability and Resilience**

   o **Explanation:** Edge computing ensures that systems can continue to operate even if connectivity to the central cloud server is lost. Since processing is done locally, devices can still function independently without being dependent on the cloud.

   o **Example:** In a remote oil rig, edge computing allows sensors to continue monitoring equipment even if there's a temporary loss of connection to the cloud. Alerts can still be generated locally, ensuring continued safety monitoring.

Challenges:

1. **Complexity in Management**
   o **Explanation:** Edge computing requires managing a distributed network of devices, which can be more complex than managing a centralized cloud-based system. Organizations must ensure that all edge devices are secure, properly maintained, and able to communicate with each other effectively.
   o **Example:** In an industrial IoT setup, managing thousands of edge devices across multiple machines and locations can become cumbersome, especially when software updates or maintenance is required.

2. **Limited Processing Power**
   o **Explanation:** While edge devices can process data locally, they typically have limited computing power compared to centralized cloud servers. This can make processing large datasets or running complex algorithms challenging at the edge.
   o **Example:** Edge devices on a factory floor may struggle to perform sophisticated machine

learning algorithms on large datasets, such as analyzing video footage from multiple cameras, without relying on the cloud for processing power.

3. **Data Synchronization and Integration**

    o **Explanation:** When data is processed locally at the edge, it can become fragmented across multiple devices. This makes it difficult to integrate and synchronize data from various edge devices with the central cloud system or other devices.

    o **Example:** In a smart city, data from various traffic sensors and streetlights processed locally might not align with data collected from other devices, making it difficult to build a unified system for traffic management.

4. **Cost of Infrastructure**

    o **Explanation:** While edge computing can reduce bandwidth costs, it may require additional investment in local infrastructure, such as edge devices, local servers, and networking equipment. This can increase initial setup costs.

    o **Example:** Deploying a network of edge devices across a large manufacturing plant to monitor equipment performance may require significant investment in hardware, software, and network infrastructure.

Real-World Scenarios Where Edge Computing Is Beneficial

Edge computing is particularly beneficial in scenarios where low latency, real-time decision-making, and local data processing are critical. Here are some real-world examples where edge computing can have a significant impact:

1. **Autonomous Vehicles**
   o **Scenario:** Autonomous vehicles rely on real-time data from sensors (such as cameras, radar, and LIDAR) to navigate roads and avoid obstacles. Processing this data in real-time at the edge (in the vehicle itself) ensures that decisions, like stopping or steering, happen without delay.
   o **Benefit:** By processing data locally, edge computing allows for faster, more reliable decision-making, which is essential for the safety of autonomous vehicles.

2. **Smart Manufacturing**
   o **Scenario:** In a smart factory, machines and sensors monitor production lines for anomalies such as temperature spikes, vibrations, or

pressure changes. Edge computing processes this data locally to trigger real-time responses, such as stopping a machine before it breaks down.

- o **Benefit:** Edge computing reduces downtime by enabling predictive maintenance and process optimization without the need to send data to the cloud, ensuring continuous production.

3. **Healthcare and Remote Patient Monitoring**

- o **Scenario:** Wearable devices and sensors can continuously monitor patient vitals such as heart rate, blood pressure, and oxygen levels. Edge computing allows for immediate analysis of this data, triggering alerts if the patient's condition requires urgent attention.

- o **Benefit:** Real-time health monitoring with edge computing ensures that patients receive immediate care when needed, even in remote areas where connectivity to the cloud might be limited.

4. **Smart Cities**

- o **Scenario:** In smart cities, traffic lights, streetlights, and environmental sensors gather real-time data to optimize traffic flow and reduce energy consumption. Edge computing processes the data locally, making instantaneous adjustments to traffic lights and other systems without needing to send data to the cloud.

- o **Benefit:** Edge computing enables quicker responses to changing conditions (such as traffic congestion) while reducing bandwidth usage and improving system reliability.

5. **Retail and Inventory Management**

- o **Scenario:** In retail stores, IoT sensors and cameras monitor inventory levels, product movement, and customer behavior. Edge computing can process this data locally, triggering actions like restocking shelves or notifying staff about product movement in real-time.
- o **Benefit:** Retailers can quickly respond to stock issues or customer needs, enhancing operational efficiency and customer satisfaction.

Edge computing is a powerful paradigm that supports IoT applications by enabling local processing, reducing latency, and improving efficiency. While it offers several advantages, it also comes with challenges that need to be managed effectively. By understanding these benefits and challenges, businesses can decide when and how to implement edge computing in their IoT ecosystems.

CHAPTER 10

SECURITY IN IOT

IoT Vulnerabilities and Risks

As IoT devices become increasingly integrated into everyday life, they also introduce a range of security vulnerabilities and risks. Since IoT devices are interconnected, they can serve as potential entry points for cyberattacks if not properly secured. Understanding these vulnerabilities is critical for designing and maintaining secure IoT systems.

1. **Weak Authentication and Authorization**
   - o **Explanation:** Many IoT devices are often shipped with default passwords or simple authentication mechanisms that are easy for attackers to exploit. Poorly implemented or absent authentication mechanisms can allow unauthorized access to IoT devices and the data they collect.
   - o **Risk:** Attackers could gain control of devices, change settings, or steal sensitive information.
   - o **Example:** Hackers could exploit default credentials on a smart home device like a camera

or thermostat, giving them remote control over the device.

2. Insecure Communication Channels

- **Explanation:** IoT devices typically communicate over wireless networks, which may be vulnerable to interception, eavesdropping, or man-in-the-middle attacks if the data transmission is not properly encrypted.

- **Risk:** Sensitive data, such as personal information or health data, can be intercepted during transmission, leading to data breaches or identity theft.

- **Example:** If a smart lock sends unencrypted communication to a mobile app, an attacker could intercept and control the lock remotely.

3. Outdated Firmware and Software

- **Explanation:** Many IoT devices run on embedded software or firmware that may not be updated regularly. Attackers can exploit known vulnerabilities in outdated firmware to compromise the device.

- **Risk:** Devices running outdated software may have unpatched security flaws, leaving them open to exploits.

- **Example:** A vulnerability in a smart TV's firmware could be exploited to gain access to the

93

device's camera or microphone, potentially spying on users.

4. Lack of Device Monitoring and Management

- o **Explanation:** Many IoT systems lack proper monitoring, making it difficult to detect abnormal behavior or potential attacks on devices.
- o **Risk:** Without adequate monitoring, malicious activities such as botnet attacks or device hijacking can go unnoticed for a long time.
- o **Example:** An IoT device could be compromised and added to a botnet, which is then used to launch a Distributed Denial of Service (DDoS) attack without the user's knowledge.

5. Insufficient Data Protection

- o **Explanation:** Many IoT devices collect large amounts of data, often sensitive in nature, such as personal, financial, or health-related information. Without proper encryption or data protection mechanisms, this data can be exposed or leaked.
- o **Risk:** Data breaches could occur, leading to identity theft, fraud, or violations of privacy.
- o **Example:** A wearable health device that tracks heart rate and location may transmit data to the cloud without encryption, making it vulnerable to hacking.

6. Physical Security Risks

94

o **Explanation:** Since IoT devices are physical objects, they can be tampered with directly if an attacker gains physical access to them. Many devices lack physical security features, making them easy targets for theft or manipulation.

o **Risk:** An attacker who gains physical access to a device could alter its functionality or install malicious software.

o **Example:** An intruder gaining access to a smart security camera could tamper with the device to disable its security features or view camera footage.

Best Practices for IoT Security

To mitigate the risks associated with IoT devices, implementing security best practices is essential. These practices help ensure the integrity, confidentiality, and availability of IoT systems and the data they handle.

1. **Strong Authentication and Access Control**

   o **Use strong, unique passwords:** Avoid default passwords and use strong, complex passwords for device authentication.

- o **Implement multi-factor authentication (MFA):** Use MFA to enhance security by requiring two or more verification methods.
- o **Role-based access control (RBAC):** Ensure that only authorized users have access to sensitive IoT devices and data, and grant permissions based on roles.

2. **Encryption of Data**

- o **Encrypt data in transit:** Use encryption protocols such as SSL/TLS to protect data transmitted between IoT devices and cloud servers.
- o **Encrypt data at rest:** Ensure that sensitive data stored on IoT devices, cloud servers, or databases is encrypted to protect it from unauthorized access.

3. **Regular Firmware and Software Updates**

- o **Update software regularly:** Ensure that IoT devices and their associated software receive timely security patches and updates.
- o **Automate firmware updates:** Where possible, configure devices to automatically install firmware updates to prevent outdated software from creating vulnerabilities.

4. **Secure Communication Protocols**

o **Use secure communication channels:** Ensure that IoT devices use secure communication protocols such as HTTPS, MQTT with TLS, or VPNs to protect data from interception.

o **Avoid open or unencrypted networks:** Do not use unencrypted protocols (e.g., HTTP, FTP) for IoT communication, especially when transmitting sensitive data.

5. IoT Device Hardening

o **Disable unnecessary services:** Disable any unused features or services on IoT devices to minimize the attack surface.

o **Enable secure boot and device verification:** Use secure boot methods that prevent unauthorized software from running on IoT devices. Implement device authentication to ensure that only authorized devices can connect to the network.

6. Monitoring and Incident Response

o **Implement continuous monitoring:** Continuously monitor IoT devices for unusual activity, signs of compromise, or data breaches.

o **Set up automated alerts:** Configure systems to automatically notify administrators of potential security issues, such as device malfunctions, network traffic anomalies, or unauthorized access attempts.

o **Develop an incident response plan:** Establish a well-defined incident response plan that outlines how to handle IoT security breaches or attacks. This plan should include steps for isolating compromised devices, conducting forensic investigations, and notifying affected parties.

Securing IoT Data and Networks

Securing IoT data and networks requires a multi-layered approach that addresses both the devices themselves and the data they generate. Here's how you can secure IoT data and networks effectively:

1. **Data Protection Techniques**
   o **Data encryption:** Ensure that all sensitive data is encrypted both in transit and at rest. This prevents unauthorized access to data if it is intercepted during transmission or stored improperly.
   o **Data minimization:** Collect only the data necessary for the functionality of IoT applications to reduce the exposure of sensitive information.
   o **Access controls:** Implement strict data access controls to ensure that only authorized users and

devices can access IoT data. Use roles and permissions to restrict access.

2. **Network Security**

- o **Segregate IoT devices on separate networks:** Use network segmentation to isolate IoT devices from critical IT systems. This reduces the risk of lateral movement in the event of a breach.

- o **Firewall protection:** Implement firewalls to monitor and control the network traffic between IoT devices, other devices, and the internet. Use intrusion detection systems (IDS) to detect abnormal behavior or potential attacks.

- o **Virtual Private Network (VPN):** Use VPNs to secure communication between IoT devices and centralized systems, especially when remote access is required.

3. **End-to-End Device Security**

- o **Device authentication:** Ensure that devices are authenticated before connecting to the network to prevent unauthorized devices from gaining access.

- o **Secure booting:** Implement secure boot processes on devices to ensure that only trusted software can run on IoT devices, preventing malicious code from being executed.

○ **Periodic security audits:** Conduct regular security audits on IoT systems to identify vulnerabilities and ensure compliance with security standards.

This chapter highlights the key vulnerabilities and risks in IoT, along with best practices for securing IoT devices and data. By following these best practices and continuously monitoring and updating IoT systems, organizations can minimize risks and ensure the security and privacy of IoT ecosystems.

CHAPTER 11

IOT IN SMART HOMES

Introduction to Smart Home Technologies

Smart homes are becoming increasingly popular as they allow homeowners to automate, control, and monitor various aspects of their home environment remotely using IoT technologies. IoT enables devices in the home to connect to the internet, communicate with each other, and be controlled via smartphones, tablets, or voice assistants like Amazon Alexa or Google Assistant. This integration of smart technologies into the home not only enhances convenience but also improves energy efficiency, security, and overall living comfort.

Key Technologies Behind Smart Homes:

1. **Sensors:** Sensors in smart home devices (e.g., motion, temperature, humidity) collect data about the environment and trigger actions such as adjusting the thermostat or turning on lights.

2. **Communication Protocols:** Communication protocols like Wi-Fi, Zigbee, Bluetooth, and Z-Wave allow devices

to interact with each other and with a central control hub, such as a smartphone or a smart speaker.

3. **Cloud and Edge Computing:** Cloud computing provides the backend infrastructure for storing and analyzing data from smart home devices, while edge computing processes data locally for real-time decision-making (e.g., turning on a light when motion is detected).

4. **Artificial Intelligence (AI) and Machine Learning:** AI and machine learning algorithms learn from user behavior and optimize home automation systems. For example, a smart thermostat may learn your heating preferences over time and adjust the temperature accordingly.

With the increasing adoption of IoT in smart homes, the landscape is rapidly evolving, offering homeowners more control, flexibility, and customization than ever before.

Real-World Smart Home Solutions

Several smart home solutions have emerged, offering users advanced automation, increased energy efficiency, and improved security. These systems integrate various IoT devices to create a cohesive and intelligent home environment.

1. **Smart Lighting Systems**

   o **Solution:** Smart lighting systems allow users to control their home's lighting remotely through apps or voice commands. These systems can be programmed to turn on or off at specific times, adjust brightness, or change colors based on mood or activity.

   o **Example:** Philips Hue smart bulbs let users adjust the lighting in any room of the house through an app. The lights can be scheduled to turn on or off automatically or dim in response to voice commands via Amazon Alexa or Google Assistant.

   o **Benefit:** Improved energy efficiency (e.g., automatically turning lights off when not needed) and enhanced convenience.

2. **Smart Thermostats**

   o **Solution:** Smart thermostats optimize the heating and cooling of a home by learning the occupants' preferences and adjusting temperatures accordingly. They can be controlled remotely via smartphone apps and can adjust settings based on occupancy or weather conditions.

   o **Example:** The Nest Learning Thermostat learns your schedule and preferences and adjusts the temperature automatically. It can also be controlled remotely through the Google Home app, ensuring your home is always at the perfect temperature when you arrive.

- o **Benefit:** Energy savings through intelligent temperature control, as well as convenience in adjusting settings remotely.

3. **Smart Security Systems**

- o **Solution:** Smart security systems include cameras, doorbell cameras, smart locks, and motion detectors that allow homeowners to monitor and control home security remotely. These devices often send real-time alerts to the user's phone when suspicious activity is detected.
- o **Example:** Ring Video Doorbell allows homeowners to see and communicate with visitors at their door remotely via their smartphone. Motion sensors and security cameras can also be integrated into the system for enhanced security.
- o **Benefit:** Enhanced home security, remote monitoring, and peace of mind with real-time alerts.

4. **Smart Plugs and Appliances**

- o **Solution:** Smart plugs and appliances allow users to control and monitor energy usage in their home. By plugging standard devices into smart plugs, users can control them remotely via an app or voice commands, and monitor power consumption.

- o **Example:** The TP-Link Kasa Smart Plug enables users to control lamps, fans, or other household devices remotely. It also provides energy usage reports to help homeowners monitor and reduce their energy consumption.
- o **Benefit:** Increased energy efficiency, remote control of devices, and improved home automation.

5. **Smart Kitchen Appliances**

- o **Solution:** Smart kitchen appliances like refrigerators, ovens, and coffee makers offer advanced features such as remote control, automated cooking settings, and personalized recipes.
- o **Example:** The Samsung Family Hub Refrigerator allows users to check the contents of their fridge remotely, create shopping lists, and even order groceries online. It also includes features like smart meal planning and recipe suggestions.
- o **Benefit:** Convenience, energy savings, and better management of kitchen tasks.

IoT Devices That Make Homes Smarter

IoT devices are the foundation of smart home systems, enabling automation, remote control, and data exchange between devices. Here's a closer look at the types of IoT devices that make homes smarter:

1. **Smart Thermostats**
    - o **Functionality:** These devices learn users' temperature preferences and schedules, automatically adjusting the heating and cooling systems for comfort and energy savings. They can be controlled remotely via apps or voice assistants.
    - o **Popular Devices:** Nest Learning Thermostat, Ecobee Smart Thermostat.

2. **Smart Lighting**
    - o **Functionality:** Smart bulbs and light switches can be controlled remotely via apps, voice assistants, or automation routines. They allow users to adjust brightness, color, and timing.
    - o **Popular Devices:** Philips Hue, LIFX, Wyze Bulbs, Sengled Smart Lighting.

3. **Smart Locks**
    - o **Functionality:** Smart locks provide keyless entry to homes and can be controlled via smartphone

apps. Some models also offer features like remote locking/unlocking, temporary access codes, and integration with home automation systems.

- o **Popular Devices:** August Smart Lock, Schlage Encode, Yale Assure Lock.

4. Smart Security Cameras

- o **Functionality:** These cameras provide real-time video surveillance of your home. They can be accessed remotely via smartphones and often include features like motion detection, night vision, and cloud storage.

- o **Popular Devices:** Ring Video Doorbell, Arlo Pro, Nest Cam IQ.

5. Smart Plugs and Outlets

- o **Functionality:** Smart plugs allow users to control the power supply to devices remotely, schedule on/off times, and monitor energy consumption. They can be plugged into standard outlets and paired with smartphones or voice assistants.

- o **Popular Devices:** TP-Link Kasa Smart Plug, Wemo Mini Smart Plug, Amazon Smart Plug.

6. Smart Doorbells

- o **Functionality:** Smart doorbells include video cameras and allow homeowners to see and speak to visitors remotely through their smartphone.

These devices also send alerts when motion is detected near the door.

- o **Popular Devices:** Ring Video Doorbell, Nest Hello, Eufy Security Video Doorbell.

7. Smart Sensors (Motion, Door/Window, and Environmental)

- o **Functionality:** Motion sensors detect movement, door/window sensors alert users to openings, and environmental sensors measure conditions like temperature, humidity, and air quality. These sensors are essential for home automation and security.

- o **Popular Devices:** Samsung SmartThings Motion Sensor, Ecobee SmartSensor, Fibaro Motion Sensor.

8. Smart Speakers and Assistants

- o **Functionality:** Smart speakers like Amazon Echo and Google Nest provide voice control for other smart devices, allowing users to manage lighting, temperature, security, and more. These devices also serve as virtual assistants for everyday tasks.

- o **Popular Devices:** Amazon Echo, Google Nest Hub, Apple HomePod.

IoT-enabled smart home solutions enhance convenience, energy efficiency, and security by allowing homeowners to control and monitor various aspects of their homes remotely. From lighting and temperature control to home security and appliances, IoT devices make everyday tasks easier, more efficient, and more enjoyable. As smart home technology continues to evolve, the possibilities for home automation will expand, providing even greater control and customization for homeowners.

CHAPTER 12

INDUSTRIAL IOT (IIOT)

The Rise of IoT in Manufacturing

The Industrial Internet of Things (IIoT) refers to the integration of IoT technologies into industrial applications, particularly manufacturing. IIoT leverages sensors, actuators, and intelligent devices to monitor, control, and optimize industrial processes. The rise of IIoT in manufacturing has transformed the industry by providing enhanced automation, real-time data collection, and improved operational efficiency.

Historically, manufacturing systems relied on manual processes and human intervention to monitor machines, detect malfunctions, and perform maintenance. However, with the proliferation of IoT technologies, sensors, and connected devices, manufacturers can now collect real-time data from equipment, machines, and the production environment. This data can be analyzed to gain valuable insights into equipment health, energy usage, and process optimization.

The rise of IIoT is driven by several factors:

1. **Advances in sensor technologies** that make it possible to collect data in real-time from various parts of the production process.

2. **Improved connectivity** with the widespread use of 5G, Wi-Fi, and low-power wide-area networks (LPWAN) that support large-scale IoT deployments.

3. **Cloud computing and data analytics** that allow manufacturers to analyze large volumes of data, identify trends, and make data-driven decisions.

4. **Cost reductions** in IoT hardware and software, making IIoT more accessible to businesses of all sizes.

5. **Increased automation**, which reduces labor costs and improves production efficiency.

IIoT is fundamentally changing how industries approach production, maintenance, and resource management by enabling real-time decision-making, predictive analytics, and smarter automation.

Key IIoT Use Cases: Predictive Maintenance, Automation

1. **Predictive Maintenance**
   o **Description:** Predictive maintenance is one of the most impactful use cases of IIoT in manufacturing. It involves using IoT sensors

to continuously monitor the health and performance of equipment in real-time. By analyzing sensor data, manufacturers can predict when a machine is likely to fail or require maintenance before it becomes a costly breakdown.

o **How It Works:** Sensors embedded in machines collect data on parameters like temperature, vibration, pressure, and humidity. This data is sent to a cloud platform or edge computing system for analysis. By applying machine learning algorithms, the system can identify patterns and anomalies that indicate potential failure. Maintenance teams are then alerted to perform maintenance before a failure occurs.

o **Benefits:**

- **Reduced downtime:** By predicting failures in advance, manufacturers can schedule maintenance when it is least disruptive to production.

- **Cost savings:** Preventing equipment failures reduces the cost of unplanned repairs and extends the lifespan of machinery.

- **Improved safety:** Predictive maintenance can help avoid dangerous situations caused by equipment malfunctions, enhancing worker safety.

o **Example:** A manufacturing plant uses vibration sensors to monitor motors and bearings in its production line. By analyzing vibration patterns, the system detects early signs of wear and alerts the maintenance team to replace parts before a breakdown occurs, preventing costly downtime.

2. **Automation and Process Optimization**

o **Description:** IIoT enables advanced automation by connecting machines, robots, and sensors across the production floor. Automated systems can perform tasks like material handling, assembly, quality inspection, and packaging, all while being monitored and controlled remotely.

o **How It Works:** Sensors and actuators are integrated with machines to enable automated processes. Data from IoT sensors is sent to control systems that adjust production processes in real-time. Additionally, robots and automated machinery can be programmed to perform repetitive tasks with precision and speed.

- ○ **Benefits:**
  - ▪ **Increased productivity:** Automation reduces the need for human intervention in repetitive tasks, speeding up production.
  - ▪ **Improved quality control:** Automated systems can monitor product quality continuously, reducing the likelihood of defects and ensuring consistency.
  - ▪ **Operational efficiency:** Real-time data collection and analysis help optimize production schedules and minimize bottlenecks.
- ○ **Example:** In an automotive manufacturing plant, robots equipped with IoT sensors handle the assembly of parts. The system continuously monitors the production process and automatically adjusts settings if deviations from the optimal process are detected, ensuring high-quality assembly and reducing human error.

3. **Energy Management**

- o **Description:** IIoT also helps manufacturers monitor and manage energy consumption across their facilities. Smart meters, sensors, and analytics platforms enable manufacturers to track energy usage in real-time, identify inefficiencies, and optimize power consumption.

- o **How It Works:** IoT-enabled energy meters and sensors provide real-time data on power usage at various points in the manufacturing process. This data is collected and analyzed to identify energy waste or areas for improvement. Automated systems can adjust equipment settings or even turn off machinery when not in use to reduce energy consumption.

- o **Benefits:**
  - **Cost savings:** Reducing energy consumption lowers operational costs, contributing to more sustainable practices.
  - **Sustainability:** Optimizing energy usage helps reduce the environmental impact of manufacturing operations.

115

- **Compliance:** Many industries are subject to regulations on energy use. IIoT systems help manufacturers meet these regulations by providing accurate data on energy consumption.

o **Example:** A large factory uses IoT sensors to monitor the energy consumption of individual machines. The system identifies machines that use more energy than necessary and suggests optimizations, such as adjusting machine settings or turning off idle machines, leading to significant energy savings.

Challenges in Implementing IIoT

While IIoT offers immense potential, there are several challenges that organizations must address when implementing these systems:

1. **Integration with Legacy Systems**
   o **Challenge:** Many manufacturing facilities still use legacy systems that were not designed to communicate with modern IoT devices.

Integrating new IoT technologies with existing infrastructure can be complex and costly.

o **Solution:** Businesses must invest in upgrading legacy systems or using middleware to bridge the gap between old and new technologies. In some cases, IIoT systems may need to be implemented in stages to ensure a smooth transition.

2. **Data Security and Privacy**

o **Challenge:** The large volume of data generated by IIoT devices raises concerns about cybersecurity. IoT devices are often vulnerable to cyberattacks, and an attack on one device can compromise the entire network.

o **Solution:** Implementing strong encryption, access controls, and network security measures is crucial to protect sensitive data and ensure the integrity of IIoT systems. Regular updates, security patches, and continuous monitoring also help mitigate security risks.

3. **Data Overload**

o **Challenge:** IIoT systems generate massive amounts of data from sensors, devices, and machines. Storing and processing this data can overwhelm IT infrastructure, leading to delays in decision-making or system crashes.

117

- o **Solution:** To manage this data overload, organizations can use edge computing to process data locally, reducing the amount of data that needs to be sent to the cloud. This helps decrease latency and improve system efficiency.

4. **Scalability**

- o **Challenge:** As IIoT systems expand, the number of devices and sensors increases, making it challenging to scale the infrastructure and maintain consistent performance.

- o **Solution:** Cloud-based IoT platforms offer scalability by providing flexible resources that can grow with the system. Additionally, IoT solutions should be designed with scalability in mind, using modular components that can be easily added or upgraded.

5. **Interoperability**

- o **Challenge:** IIoT systems often involve devices and sensors from multiple vendors, which may use different communication protocols or standards. Ensuring that these devices can communicate effectively with one another is a major challenge.

- o **Solution:** Adopting open standards and using middleware platforms that enable communication between devices from different manufacturers can help improve interoperability. Additionally, cloud platforms like Microsoft Azure IoT and AWS IoT provide solutions for integrating diverse IoT devices into a cohesive system.

IIoT is revolutionizing manufacturing by enabling predictive maintenance, automation, energy management, and real-time optimization. However, successful implementation requires addressing key challenges such as legacy system integration, data security, and scalability. By carefully planning and addressing these challenges, manufacturers can unlock the full potential of IIoT to improve operational efficiency and competitiveness.

CHAPTER 13

IOT IN HEALTHCARE

Remote Monitoring and Telemedicine

The integration of IoT into healthcare has significantly enhanced the way patients are monitored and treated. One of the most impactful applications of IoT in healthcare is **remote monitoring**, where patients' health data is continuously collected and transmitted to healthcare providers, enabling timely interventions without the need for frequent in-person visits. This is especially useful for patients with chronic conditions, elderly individuals, and those living in remote areas.

1. **Remote Monitoring**
    o **Description:** Remote monitoring involves using IoT devices to collect patient data, such as vital signs (e.g., heart rate, blood pressure, glucose levels) or even more complex metrics (e.g., ECG readings). This data is transmitted to healthcare providers or medical systems in real-time, allowing for continuous monitoring and early detection of potential health issues.
    o **Examples:**

120

- **Wearable ECG Monitors:** Devices like **Apple Watch** or **AliveCor KardiaMobile** can monitor the heart's electrical activity and alert patients or doctors to irregularities, such as arrhythmias.

- **Blood Glucose Monitors:** Devices like **Dexcom** or **Freestyle Libre** continuously monitor blood sugar levels in diabetic patients and transmit data to a mobile app, allowing for real-time adjustments to insulin doses.

- **Blood Pressure Monitors:** IoT-enabled blood pressure monitors can automatically send readings to a healthcare provider, ensuring that patients with hypertension receive timely advice and treatment.

o **Benefits:**

- **Convenience:** Patients can receive healthcare services remotely, reducing the need for frequent hospital visits and saving time.

- **Continuous Monitoring:** Healthcare providers can monitor patients' health data in real-time, improving early detection and reducing emergency situations.

- **Cost Savings:** Remote monitoring reduces the need for expensive in-person visits and hospital admissions.

2. Telemedicine

- **Description:** Telemedicine refers to the remote diagnosis and treatment of patients using telecommunications technology, including video calls, secure messaging, and remote monitoring devices. IoT enhances telemedicine by providing the tools needed to monitor patients' conditions continuously and relay that information to healthcare providers.

- **Examples:**
  - **Video Consultations:** Healthcare providers can use video conferencing tools to consult with patients, offering immediate advice and prescriptions.
  - **Remote Diagnostics:** IoT devices can capture diagnostic data (e.g., thermometers, pulse oximeters) and send it to a doctor for analysis. The doctor can then provide a diagnosis or treatment plan based on the transmitted data.

- **Benefits:**

- **Access to Healthcare:** Telemedicine helps patients in remote or underserved areas access healthcare services.
- **Convenience and Comfort:** Patients can receive medical care from the comfort of their homes, especially for minor ailments or follow-up appointments.
- **Timely Interventions:** IoT and telemedicine together ensure that patients receive the care they need without delays.

Wearables and IoT Devices in Health Applications

Wearables and other IoT devices are increasingly being used in healthcare for a variety of applications. These devices enable continuous monitoring of a patient's health metrics, allowing for better management of chronic conditions, improved patient engagement, and enhanced health outcomes.

1. **Wearables**
   - **Description:** Wearable devices are small, portable electronics that can be worn on the body to monitor a wide range of health metrics. These

devices are equipped with sensors that collect data about the user's body and environment, which can then be transmitted to mobile apps or healthcare providers.

- o **Examples:**
  - **Fitness Trackers:** Devices like **Fitbit**, **Garmin**, and **Xiaomi Mi Band** track physical activity, heart rate, sleep patterns, and other metrics, providing users with valuable insights into their health and fitness.
  - **Smartwatches:** Devices like the **Apple Watch** and **Samsung Galaxy Watch** not only track fitness metrics but also monitor more complex health data, including heart rate variability, ECG, and blood oxygen levels. They can send alerts if irregularities are detected, helping users monitor their heart health.
  - **Wearable ECG Monitors: AliveCor KardiaMobile** allows users to perform ECG tests at home and share the results with their healthcare provider for analysis.
- o **Benefits:**

124

- **Health Tracking:** Wearables provide continuous health monitoring, helping individuals track their wellness goals and detect early signs of health issues.

- **Early Intervention:** Devices that monitor heart rate, blood pressure, and glucose levels help identify irregularities, enabling early intervention and potentially reducing the risk of serious conditions like heart disease or stroke.

- **Convenience:** Wearables are often non-invasive and can be worn throughout the day, allowing users to track their health without disruption.

2. **Other IoT Devices in Healthcare**

   o **Smart Inhalers:** IoT-enabled inhalers help asthma patients by tracking their medication usage and ensuring they adhere to prescribed regimens. Devices like **Propeller Health** transmit data to a smartphone app, which then provides feedback to both the patient and healthcare provider.

   o **Smart Bed Sensors:** Hospitals and care facilities use IoT sensors embedded in beds to monitor patient movement, detect falls, and ensure that patients are positioned comfortably, reducing the risk of pressure ulcers or other complications.

- o **Wearable Pulse Oximeters:** Devices like **Wellue** and **Masimo** monitor oxygen saturation levels, which is essential for patients with respiratory conditions like COPD or COVID-19. These devices can alert users or healthcare providers to low oxygen levels.
- o **Smart Pill Bottles:** IoT-enabled pill bottles like **Tespo** help patients stay on track with their medication schedules by sending reminders and tracking medication usage.

IoT-Driven Health Outcomes and Case Studies

The use of IoT in healthcare is resulting in significant improvements in patient outcomes, healthcare delivery, and cost-effectiveness. By enabling continuous monitoring and facilitating early interventions, IoT technologies help prevent complications, reduce hospital readmissions, and improve overall health.

1. **Case Study 1: Chronic Disease Management**
   - o **Scenario:** A study of diabetes management using IoT devices highlighted the success of continuous

glucose monitoring (CGM) systems in improving patient outcomes. Devices like **Dexcom G6** and **Freestyle Libre** provide real-time glucose readings and send them to patients' smartphones.

o **Outcome:** Patients with diabetes who used CGM systems saw improved blood glucose control and fewer complications. Remote monitoring also allowed healthcare providers to adjust treatment plans in real-time, reducing the need for frequent in-person visits.

o **Impact:** This led to better management of diabetes, fewer hospitalizations, and improved quality of life for patients.

2. **Case Study 2: Remote Cardiac Monitoring**

o **Scenario:** In a study of heart disease management, wearable devices like the **Apple Watch** were used to monitor patients' heart rate, ECG, and blood oxygen levels remotely. Patients with a history of heart disease wore the device, which transmitted health data to healthcare providers.

o **Outcome:** The real-time monitoring allowed doctors to detect arrhythmias and other heart conditions early, enabling immediate intervention. Patients were more engaged in their care, as they could track their heart health continuously.

- o **Impact:** The use of wearables reduced emergency hospital visits and heart-related complications, ultimately saving healthcare costs and improving patient satisfaction.

3. **Case Study 3: Post-Surgery Recovery**

- o **Scenario:** In a hospital setting, IoT-enabled smart beds were used to monitor patient movement and vitals after surgery. Sensors tracked patient activity, sleep patterns, and heart rate, sending the data to the hospital's central system.

- o **Outcome:** The system helped detect early signs of complications, such as deep vein thrombosis (DVT), by monitoring for signs of immobility or irregular vitals. It also helped staff ensure that patients were positioned properly to prevent pressure ulcers.

- o **Impact:** The smart bed system improved patient recovery, reduced complications, and increased operational efficiency by alerting healthcare staff to potential issues in real-time.

IoT is transforming healthcare by enabling real-time monitoring, enhancing patient engagement, and improving the efficiency of healthcare delivery. From wearables and telemedicine to predictive health analytics, IoT technologies are driving better health outcomes, making healthcare more accessible, and reducing costs.

CHAPTER 14

IOT FOR SMART CITIES

IoT Applications in Urban Planning and Infrastructure

The integration of IoT technologies into urban planning and infrastructure is transforming cities into smarter, more efficient, and more sustainable environments. IoT systems can collect and analyze data from various urban elements—such as traffic, utilities, and public services—helping city planners and officials make informed decisions, optimize resource use, and improve the quality of life for residents. Below are key applications of IoT in urban planning and infrastructure:

1. **Urban Data Collection and Analysis**
   - **Description:** IoT devices are used to gather data from various sensors embedded in cities, such as air quality sensors, traffic cameras, noise detectors, and waste bins. The collected data is transmitted to central platforms for analysis, enabling better city management and planning.
   - **Examples:**
     - **Air Quality Monitoring:** IoT sensors can continuously monitor air quality and

pollution levels, providing real-time data on harmful emissions. This data helps city officials take actions to improve public health by adjusting traffic patterns or regulating industrial emissions.

- **Smart Street Lighting:** IoT-enabled streetlights use sensors to detect ambient light levels and human presence, adjusting brightness based on real-time conditions to optimize energy consumption and enhance safety.

2. **Smart Infrastructure Management**

- o **Description:** Infrastructure such as bridges, roads, and buildings can be equipped with IoT sensors that monitor their condition in real-time. These sensors detect wear and tear, cracks, temperature changes, or vibrations, providing data to predict maintenance needs and prevent accidents or failures.

- o **Examples:**

  - **Bridge and Roadway Monitoring:** Sensors embedded in bridges and highways monitor structural integrity, detecting potential issues such as cracks or shifts in alignment. Early detection of damage enables preventive maintenance,

131

extending the lifespan of infrastructure and ensuring public safety.

Smart Traffic, Waste Management, and Energy Efficiency

Smart cities use IoT technologies to optimize traffic flow, improve waste management processes, and enhance energy efficiency. These applications aim to make cities more livable, sustainable, and cost-effective.

1. **Smart Traffic Management**
   o **Description:** IoT enables real-time traffic monitoring and management by collecting data from sensors, cameras, and GPS devices in vehicles. This data is used to optimize traffic flow, reduce congestion, and improve safety on the roads.
   o **Examples:**
     ▪ **Adaptive Traffic Signals:** IoT-enabled traffic signals can adjust in real-time based on the volume of traffic, ensuring smoother flow and reducing congestion. For example, when a traffic camera detects heavy traffic at a particular intersection, the signal can automatically stay green longer to clear traffic.

132

- **Smart Parking:** IoT sensors in parking spaces monitor their availability, sending real-time data to a central system. Drivers can access this information through apps, helping them find available parking spots quickly and reducing unnecessary traffic on city streets.

  o **Benefits:**
    - **Reduced Traffic Congestion:** Real-time traffic management leads to fewer traffic jams, quicker travel times, and reduced fuel consumption.
    - **Improved Road Safety:** Smart traffic management systems can reduce accidents by adjusting traffic signals based on real-time data, such as congestion or accidents.

2. **Smart Waste Management**
   o **Description:** IoT technologies enable more efficient waste collection and management. Sensors in waste bins monitor fill levels, and data from these sensors is used to optimize waste collection routes and schedules, ensuring that bins are emptied when they are full and reducing unnecessary collection trips.
   o **Examples:**

133

- **Smart Bins:** IoT-enabled waste bins equipped with sensors can send alerts when they are full, allowing waste collection teams to plan their routes accordingly and optimize fuel use. These bins can also monitor the type of waste being disposed of, contributing to more efficient recycling programs.
- **Waste Sorting:** IoT sensors can help improve the sorting of recyclable materials by monitoring waste content in real-time, ensuring that recyclable materials are separated from regular trash and sent to appropriate facilities.

o **Benefits:**

- **Cost Efficiency:** Optimized waste collection schedules reduce fuel consumption and labor costs for waste management services.
- **Sustainability:** More efficient recycling and waste collection processes help reduce environmental impact by promoting recycling and reducing unnecessary waste transportation.

3. **Smart Energy Efficiency**

o **Description:** IoT systems help cities manage their energy consumption more effectively by optimizing the use of electricity, water, and heating. Sensors monitor energy usage patterns and make adjustments to improve efficiency and reduce waste.

o **Examples:**

- **Smart Grids:** IoT sensors in the electrical grid provide real-time data on power usage, allowing utilities to predict demand and balance the load. Smart grids also support decentralized energy generation, such as solar and wind, by integrating data from renewable energy sources.

- **Energy-Efficient Buildings:** IoT devices in buildings monitor lighting, temperature, and HVAC systems, adjusting them based on occupancy and usage patterns. This reduces energy consumption and lowers utility costs.

o **Benefits:**

- **Energy Savings:** By optimizing energy consumption, smart city systems help reduce the overall demand for electricity,

135

leading to cost savings and environmental benefits.

- **Sustainability:** IoT-driven energy efficiency initiatives contribute to reducing carbon emissions, making cities more sustainable and reducing their environmental footprint.

Real-World Smart City Projects

Several cities around the world have already begun implementing IoT solutions to enhance urban living and improve efficiency. Here are some notable real-world examples of smart city projects that leverage IoT technologies:

1. **Barcelona, Spain**
   - **Overview:** Barcelona has become one of the world's leading smart cities, with a focus on improving sustainability, mobility, and governance through IoT technologies. The city uses IoT solutions for smart lighting, waste management, parking, and air quality monitoring.
   - **Key Features:**

- **Smart Parking:** IoT sensors in parking spaces provide real-time data on availability, helping drivers find parking more efficiently.
- **Smart Lighting:** The city uses energy-efficient streetlights that adjust brightness based on movement or ambient light, reducing energy consumption.
- **Environmental Monitoring:** IoT sensors monitor air quality, providing data on pollution levels and helping the city implement policies to improve air quality.

  o **Impact:** Barcelona's IoT infrastructure has reduced energy consumption, improved traffic flow, and helped the city become more sustainable.

2. **Singapore**

  o **Overview:** Singapore has developed one of the most comprehensive smart city initiatives, incorporating IoT into urban planning, transportation, and waste management. The city's aim is to become a "smart nation" by using technology to improve citizens' quality of life.

  o **Key Features:**

- **Smart Traffic Management:** IoT-enabled cameras and sensors monitor traffic conditions in real-time and adjust traffic light timings to reduce congestion.
- **Smart Waste Management:** Sensors in trash bins notify waste collection teams when bins are full, optimizing collection routes and schedules.
- **Public Safety and Security:** IoT-enabled surveillance cameras and sensors help monitor public spaces for safety, providing real-time data to authorities.
  - **Impact:** The use of IoT in Singapore has led to better traffic management, improved public safety, and more efficient use of urban resources.

3. **Songdo, South Korea**
   - **Overview:** Songdo is a planned smart city built from the ground up, designed to be a model for future urban development. The city incorporates a wide range of IoT solutions, including smart infrastructure, waste management, and energy efficiency.
   - **Key Features:**
     - **Smart Buildings:** Buildings in Songdo are equipped with IoT sensors to monitor temperature, lighting, and energy usage.

138

Smart systems automatically adjust settings to optimize energy efficiency.

- **Waste Management:** The city uses a pneumatic waste collection system that transports waste through underground pipes to a central facility for processing, reducing the need for traditional waste trucks.

- **Smart Healthcare:** IoT-enabled health monitoring devices allow residents to track vital signs and connect with healthcare providers remotely.

- **Impact:** Songdo serves as a showcase for integrating IoT into urban design, improving residents' quality of life, reducing energy consumption, and optimizing waste management.

IoT is playing a crucial role in the development of smart cities by enabling efficient management of urban resources, improving sustainability, and enhancing citizens' overall well-being. From smart traffic systems to waste management and energy efficiency, IoT technologies are helping cities become more livable, sustainable, and resilient.

CHAPTER 15

ENERGY EFFICIENCY AND IOT

IoT's Role in Energy Management and Sustainability

The integration of IoT technologies into energy management systems is playing a pivotal role in driving sustainability and improving energy efficiency across various sectors. IoT enables real-time monitoring, control, and optimization of energy consumption, providing both individuals and organizations with the tools to make smarter, more informed decisions about their energy use. Through the collection and analysis of vast amounts of data from sensors and devices, IoT contributes to reducing waste, lowering energy costs, and supporting the transition toward more sustainable practices.

1. **Real-Time Monitoring**

    o **How It Works:** IoT devices such as smart meters, sensors, and connected appliances collect real-time data on energy consumption from homes, buildings, factories, and entire cities. This data is transmitted to central systems where it can be analyzed to identify patterns, peak usage times, and inefficiencies.

- o **Benefits:** Real-time monitoring allows for immediate adjustments to energy consumption, reducing waste and ensuring that energy is used more efficiently.

2. **Automated Energy Management**

- o **How It Works:** With IoT-enabled automation, energy systems can autonomously adjust settings based on real-time data. For example, smart thermostats can adjust heating and cooling based on occupancy, while smart lighting systems can dim or turn off lights when rooms are not in use.

- o **Benefits:** Automation reduces the need for manual intervention, increases comfort, and significantly lowers energy consumption, especially in commercial and residential buildings.

3. **Predictive Analytics for Energy Optimization**

- o **How It Works:** IoT devices collect data over time, allowing for predictive analytics to forecast energy demand and optimize usage patterns. Machine learning algorithms can identify inefficiencies and recommend changes to improve energy use.

- o **Benefits:** Predictive analytics help organizations and individuals reduce energy waste by anticipating demand and adjusting energy usage

141

proactively. This leads to lower operational costs and supports environmental sustainability goals.

4. **Supporting Renewable Energy Integration**

   o **How It Works:** IoT plays a critical role in integrating renewable energy sources, such as solar and wind, into the grid. Sensors and smart devices can monitor energy production and consumption, ensuring that energy is stored or distributed efficiently to meet demand.

   o **Benefits:** The integration of renewable energy into the grid helps reduce dependency on fossil fuels, lowering carbon emissions and promoting a more sustainable energy infrastructure.

Smart Grids, Meters, and Energy Conservation

Smart grids, smart meters, and energy conservation technologies are essential components of an IoT-enabled energy management system. These technologies improve the efficiency, reliability, and sustainability of energy distribution and consumption.

1. **Smart Grids**

   o **Description:** A smart grid is an advanced energy distribution network that uses IoT technology to collect real-time data from sensors and meters distributed across the grid. The system uses this data to monitor energy flow, optimize distribution, and prevent energy loss.

- **How It Works:** Smart grids utilize two-way communication between energy providers and consumers. This communication allows for dynamic adjustments based on current demand, weather conditions, or grid congestion. For example, during high demand periods, the smart grid can automatically switch to backup energy sources or adjust the flow to different regions to balance the load.

- **Benefits:**
  - **Increased Efficiency:** Real-time data helps balance supply and demand, reducing energy waste and enhancing grid reliability.
  - **Reduced Downtime:** Smart grids can quickly detect and respond to faults or failures, minimizing downtime and service disruptions.
  - **Integration of Renewable Energy:** Smart grids allow for efficient integration of renewable energy sources,

143

such as wind and solar power, into the main energy grid.

2. **Smart Meters**

o **Description:** Smart meters are devices that record energy consumption in real-time and send the data to energy providers. They replace traditional analog meters, providing consumers with more accurate and timely data on their energy use.

o **How It Works:** Smart meters transmit data through secure communication networks to utilities, allowing them to monitor usage patterns, detect anomalies, and manage energy distribution more effectively. Consumers can also access their usage data through apps or online dashboards, giving them better control over their energy consumption.

o **Benefits:**

▪ **Accurate Billing:** Smart meters provide accurate, real-time data, eliminating the need for estimated readings and ensuring consumers are only billed for the energy they actually use.

▪ **Energy Conservation:** Consumers can track their energy usage and make informed decisions to reduce

144

consumption, such as adjusting thermostat settings or turning off unused devices.

- **Dynamic Pricing:** Utilities can implement dynamic pricing based on demand, encouraging consumers to use energy during off-peak hours and helping to balance the grid.

3. **Energy Conservation Systems**

   o **Description:** IoT-enabled energy conservation systems use sensors and automated controls to monitor and reduce energy consumption in buildings, factories, and public spaces.

   o **How It Works:** IoT sensors detect occupancy, temperature, and lighting conditions, and use this data to adjust heating, cooling, and lighting systems accordingly. Smart HVAC systems, for example, can learn a building's usage patterns and adjust settings to minimize energy consumption while maintaining comfort.

   o **Benefits:**
     - **Cost Savings:** By optimizing energy use, these systems help organizations and homeowners reduce energy bills.
     - **Improved Sustainability:** Energy conservation systems reduce carbon

145

footprints by ensuring that energy is used only when and where it is needed.

- **Enhanced Comfort:** Automated adjustments to lighting, heating, and cooling improve the comfort of building occupants while conserving energy.

Case Studies of Energy-Efficient IoT Solutions

The integration of IoT solutions for energy efficiency has been implemented in several real-world projects across various industries, demonstrating the potential of IoT to drive sustainability and cost savings.

1. **Case Study 1: Smart Grid in Boulder, Colorado (USA)**

   o **Overview:** The city of Boulder implemented a smart grid project that included IoT-enabled sensors, smart meters, and automated systems for real-time energy monitoring and management.

   o **Solution:** The smart grid integrated renewable energy sources, such as solar and wind power, with traditional energy sources, ensuring that energy was distributed efficiently across the city. Smart meters were installed in homes and businesses, providing residents with real-time data on their energy consumption.

- o **Outcome:** The project resulted in improved energy efficiency, a reduction in carbon emissions, and better integration of renewable energy. The real-time data also allowed for better grid management, reducing outages and improving the overall reliability of the energy system.

2. **Case Study 2: Smart Buildings in Toronto, Canada**

- o **Overview:** The city of Toronto implemented IoT-based energy management systems in its municipal buildings to reduce energy consumption and improve sustainability.

- o **Solution:** IoT sensors were installed in HVAC systems, lighting, and other building systems to monitor energy use. The system adjusted energy consumption based on occupancy and real-time data, ensuring that energy was used efficiently.

- o **Outcome:** Energy consumption was reduced by 15%, resulting in significant cost savings and a reduction in the environmental impact of municipal buildings. The system also enabled real-time monitoring and predictive maintenance, further improving efficiency and sustainability.

3. **Case Study 3: Energy-Efficient Manufacturing in Germany**

   o **Overview:** A manufacturing plant in Germany implemented IoT solutions to monitor and optimize energy use across its production lines.

   o **Solution:** The plant installed IoT sensors on machines to monitor energy usage and identify inefficiencies. The system analyzed energy data and provided actionable insights to reduce power consumption without compromising production.

   o **Outcome:** The system led to a 20% reduction in energy costs by optimizing machine usage, scheduling energy-intensive processes during off-peak hours, and adjusting settings to minimize power consumption. The plant also improved its sustainability by reducing carbon emissions.

IoT is revolutionizing energy management by enabling real-time monitoring, optimization, and conservation of energy. From smart grids and meters to energy-efficient buildings and industrial applications, IoT technologies help reduce waste, lower costs, and promote sustainability. As cities, businesses, and homeowners continue to adopt IoT solutions, the potential for energy savings and environmental benefits will grow exponentially.

CHAPTER 16

THE ROLE OF ARTIFICIAL INTELLIGENCE (AI) IN IOT

How AI Complements IoT

The combination of Artificial Intelligence (AI) and the Internet of Things (IoT) is creating intelligent systems capable of learning, decision-making, and automating processes without human intervention. IoT devices collect vast amounts of data, but it's AI that allows this data to be processed, analyzed, and transformed into actionable insights, enabling smarter decision-making and optimized operations.

1. **Data Processing and Analysis**

    o   **Role of AI:** IoT devices generate enormous volumes of data, but raw data alone isn't useful without proper analysis. AI algorithms, particularly machine learning (ML) and deep learning, can analyze this data in real-time, identifying patterns, trends, and anomalies that would be difficult for humans to spot. This allows for smarter, more informed decisions.

- o **Example:** In a smart factory, IoT sensors monitor machine performance, collecting data on temperature, vibration, and speed. AI analyzes this data to predict when a machine will fail, enabling predictive maintenance that reduces downtime.

2. **Decision Making and Predictive Insights**

- o **Role of AI:** AI doesn't just process data—it can make predictions and decisions based on historical data and patterns. This is particularly useful in situations where time-sensitive decisions are required, such as in healthcare, autonomous vehicles, or energy management.

- o **Example:** In healthcare, IoT-enabled wearable devices collect real-time health data (heart rate, blood pressure, etc.), which AI algorithms analyze to detect potential health risks and alert healthcare providers or the patient immediately.

3. **AI-Enhanced Automation**

- o **Role of AI:** AI allows IoT systems to become more autonomous, reducing the need for manual intervention. This is especially valuable in applications like smart cities, home automation, and industrial operations, where AI can optimize performance, reduce inefficiencies, and enhance overall system functionality.

- o **Example:** In a smart home, IoT sensors collect data on temperature, lighting, and occupancy, while AI algorithms learn the user's preferences. Based on this information, the system can automatically adjust lighting, temperature, and other factors without the user having to make adjustments manually.

AI-Driven Automation in IoT Systems

AI-driven automation is one of the most powerful applications of IoT, enabling devices to not only monitor their environments but also take proactive actions based on the insights derived from AI algorithms. This synergy is changing how industries operate, improving efficiency, reducing errors, and optimizing processes.

1. **Autonomous Vehicles**
   - o **How AI and IoT Work Together:** IoT sensors (cameras, radar, LIDAR) in autonomous vehicles collect real-time data about the vehicle's surroundings. AI processes this data to make decisions, such as detecting pedestrians, other vehicles, and road hazards, and then taking actions like braking or steering.

152

o **Automation Example:** An autonomous vehicle uses IoT sensors to monitor its environment and AI to make decisions about acceleration, braking, and lane changes, all without human intervention.

2. **Smart Manufacturing and Industry 4.0**

   o **How AI and IoT Work Together:** In manufacturing, IoT devices are used to collect data on equipment performance, inventory levels, and supply chain conditions. AI algorithms process this data to identify inefficiencies, forecast production needs, and optimize the flow of materials.

   o **Automation Example:** An AI-driven system in a smart factory automatically adjusts production schedules, orders raw materials, and performs predictive maintenance on equipment, all without manual input. This helps to increase productivity and minimize downtime.

3. **Smart Homes and Building Automation**

   o **How AI and IoT Work Together:** In smart homes, IoT sensors monitor various parameters like temperature, humidity, occupancy, and energy usage. AI systems analyze this data and automate actions, such as adjusting heating or cooling, controlling lights, or locking doors based on the time of day or the occupants' preferences.

- o **Automation Example:** In a smart home, AI learns when to adjust the thermostat, turn off lights, or lock doors, improving energy efficiency and convenience for residents.

4. **Smart Agriculture**

- o **How AI and IoT Work Together:** IoT sensors monitor environmental conditions such as soil moisture, temperature, and light levels. AI algorithms process this data to optimize irrigation schedules, plant growth conditions, and pest management.

- o **Automation Example:** A farm uses IoT sensors to monitor soil conditions, while AI systems analyze this data to automatically adjust irrigation schedules based on real-time weather data and soil moisture levels, optimizing water usage and improving crop yields.

Case Examples of AI and IoT Integration

The integration of AI and IoT is already having a transformative effect in several industries. Below are some notable real-world examples where AI and IoT are combined to drive automation, improve efficiency, and create innovative solutions.

1. **Case Example 1: Predictive Maintenance in Manufacturing**
   - **Scenario:** In a large manufacturing plant, IoT sensors are embedded in machines to monitor variables like temperature, vibration, and pressure. The data is sent to a cloud platform where AI algorithms analyze it to predict when a machine will require maintenance or is likely to fail.
   - **Outcome:** By using AI to analyze IoT data, the company can perform predictive maintenance on machinery, reducing unexpected downtime and extending the lifespan of equipment. This leads to significant cost savings and improved production efficiency.
   - **Technology Used:** AI-powered predictive analytics, IoT sensors, and cloud computing.

2. **Case Example 2: AI-Driven Traffic Management in Smart Cities**
   - **Scenario:** In a smart city, IoT sensors monitor traffic flow, vehicle speed, and congestion levels in real-time. AI algorithms process this data to optimize traffic lights, manage congestion, and provide real-time traffic alerts to drivers.
   - **Outcome:** By analyzing real-time traffic data, the city can reduce traffic congestion, improve traffic

155

flow, and minimize carbon emissions. AI-driven traffic systems help make cities more efficient and livable.

- o **Technology Used:** IoT-enabled traffic sensors, AI-powered traffic management systems, and real-time data analytics.

3. **Case Example 3: AI in Healthcare – Wearable Health Devices**

    - o **Scenario:** Wearable health devices, such as fitness trackers and smartwatches, use IoT sensors to monitor vital signs like heart rate, blood pressure, and oxygen levels. AI algorithms analyze this data to detect potential health risks and provide real-time alerts to users or healthcare providers.

    - o **Outcome:** These AI-powered devices provide early warnings for conditions like arrhythmias, heart disease, or dehydration, allowing users to seek medical attention before conditions worsen. This proactive health management leads to better health outcomes and fewer emergency visits.

    - o **Technology Used:** Wearable IoT devices, AI-driven health analytics, and machine learning algorithms for predictive healthcare.

4. **Case Example 4: AI and IoT in Agriculture – Smart Farming**

- **Scenario:** In smart farming, IoT devices such as soil sensors, weather stations, and drones collect data about environmental conditions. AI algorithms analyze this data to optimize irrigation, fertilization, and pest control.

- **Outcome:** AI-driven IoT systems help farmers make data-driven decisions that reduce water usage, optimize fertilizer application, and improve crop yields. This leads to more sustainable farming practices and higher productivity.

- **Technology Used:** IoT sensors for environmental monitoring, AI-based predictive analytics, and automation in farming operations.

The integration of AI and IoT has revolutionized industries by enabling automation, enhancing efficiency, and creating smarter, more responsive systems. Whether in manufacturing, smart cities, healthcare, or agriculture, AI and IoT together are optimizing operations and providing significant benefits in cost savings, sustainability, and overall performance. As AI technology continues to advance, its synergy with IoT will only become more integral in shaping the future of industries worldwide.

157

CHAPTER 17

IOT FOR AGRICULTURE

Smart Farming and Precision Agriculture

IoT has revolutionized agriculture by enabling **smart farming** and **precision agriculture**, two practices that leverage technology to optimize farming processes, increase crop yields, reduce costs, and promote sustainability. These approaches allow farmers to make data-driven decisions, improving efficiency and minimizing resource waste.

1. **Smart Farming**

   o **Description:** Smart farming refers to the integration of IoT technologies into farming practices to automate, monitor, and control agricultural operations. It involves using IoT devices to collect data from various environmental and operational parameters, which is then analyzed to make informed decisions and optimize farming practices.

   o **Key Components:**

      ▪ **Automation:** IoT devices can automate processes such as irrigation, fertilization, and crop harvesting based on real-time data.

- **Monitoring:** IoT-enabled sensors collect data about soil moisture, temperature, humidity, and pest activity to optimize environmental conditions for crop growth.

- **Remote Control:** Farmers can control and monitor systems remotely, ensuring constant optimization of farming conditions even without being physically present on-site.

2. **Precision Agriculture**

    o **Description:** Precision agriculture is an approach that uses IoT technologies to optimize field-level management. By collecting and analyzing data on crop conditions, weather, and soil, precision agriculture allows farmers to tailor their practices to the specific needs of their crops, resulting in higher yields and reduced resource use.

    o **Key Components:**

        - **Variable Rate Technology (VRT):** VRT allows farmers to apply water, fertilizers, and pesticides at varying rates across their fields, depending on real-time soil and crop conditions.

159

- **Geospatial Analysis:** GPS-enabled devices track precise locations of farm equipment and optimize the movement and operation of agricultural machinery.
- **Data-Driven Decisions:** Data from IoT sensors and other connected devices is analyzed to determine the best time for planting, irrigation, fertilization, and harvesting.

IoT Devices Used in Agriculture (Drones, Soil Sensors)

Several IoT devices are being used to improve efficiency and productivity in agriculture. These devices help monitor crop health, manage resources more efficiently, and automate various tasks, making farming more sustainable and cost-effective.

1. **Drones**
   - **Description:** Drones are equipped with cameras, sensors, and GPS systems that allow farmers to collect high-resolution aerial imagery of their fields. Drones provide valuable data on crop health, soil conditions, and overall field performance.

o **How They Work:** Drones fly over fields and capture data through multi-spectral, thermal, or RGB cameras. They create detailed maps that allow farmers to assess plant health, monitor irrigation systems, and detect pest infestations.

o **Benefits:**

- **Crop Health Monitoring:** Drones can detect issues like nutrient deficiencies, water stress, and pest infestations by analyzing the images they capture. This enables early intervention to prevent crop loss.

- **Precision Spraying:** Drones can also be used to apply fertilizers and pesticides in specific areas of the field, reducing chemical use and improving efficiency.

2. **Soil Sensors**

o **Description:** Soil sensors are embedded in the ground to monitor key soil parameters like moisture levels, temperature, pH, and nutrient content. These sensors provide real-time data that helps farmers understand the soil conditions and adjust irrigation, fertilization, and other practices accordingly.

o **How They Work:** Soil sensors collect data on soil moisture, temperature, and nutrient levels.

The information is sent to cloud platforms or apps where farmers can access real-time insights and make adjustments.

- o **Benefits:**
  - **Efficient Irrigation:** By monitoring soil moisture levels in real-time, IoT-enabled soil sensors ensure that crops receive just the right amount of water, reducing water waste and improving crop health.
  - **Fertilization Optimization:** Sensors can measure the availability of nutrients in the soil, helping farmers apply fertilizers only where and when they are needed, reducing costs and environmental impact.

3. **Weather Stations**
   - o **Description:** IoT-enabled weather stations provide real-time data on weather conditions such as temperature, humidity, wind speed, and precipitation levels. This data is used to predict weather patterns, optimize irrigation schedules, and plan for extreme weather events.
   - o **How They Work:** Sensors installed at various locations in a field collect weather data and transmit it to central systems or cloud platforms,

where it is analyzed and used to inform farming decisions.

- o **Benefits:**
  - **Microclimate Monitoring:** Weather stations provide localized weather data, helping farmers understand specific conditions on their fields and adjust practices accordingly.
  - **Climate-Resilient Planning:** Data from weather stations can help farmers predict and prepare for weather-related challenges, such as droughts, frost, or storms.

4. Livestock Monitoring Systems

- o **Description:** IoT devices for livestock monitoring track the health, location, and behavior of animals. These devices use sensors and RFID technology to collect data on animals, enabling farmers to monitor their herds and improve animal welfare.
- o **How They Work:** Wearable devices and sensors attached to livestock collect data on temperature, movement, and feeding behavior. This data is transmitted to a central system for analysis, helping farmers detect early signs of illness or distress.

o **Benefits:**

- **Health Monitoring:** By continuously monitoring vital signs and activity levels, farmers can quickly identify sick animals and take corrective action, reducing disease spread and improving overall herd health.

- **Improved Productivity:** IoT-based livestock monitoring improves breeding, feeding, and healthcare management, ultimately boosting livestock productivity.

Benefits and Real-World Implementations

The adoption of IoT technologies in agriculture has provided numerous benefits, from improving crop yields to reducing resource usage and enhancing sustainability. Below are some key benefits and real-world examples of IoT applications in agriculture:

1. **Increased Crop Yields**

   o **Benefit:** By using IoT sensors to monitor environmental conditions in real-time, farmers can make more informed decisions that help optimize growing conditions for crops, leading to higher yields.

- o **Example:** In precision agriculture, farmers use soil moisture sensors and weather data to optimize irrigation schedules, ensuring that crops receive the right amount of water at the right time. This results in better crop growth and higher yields with less water.

2. **Resource Efficiency and Sustainability**

- o **Benefit:** IoT systems enable more efficient use of resources like water, fertilizer, and pesticides. By applying these resources based on real-time data, farmers can minimize waste, reduce costs, and decrease the environmental impact of farming.

- o **Example:** The **CropX** soil sensor system monitors soil conditions and provides farmers with insights on when and where to apply irrigation or fertilizers, reducing water usage and minimizing chemical runoff into the environment.

3. **Reduced Operational Costs**

- o **Benefit:** Automation and data-driven decision-making reduce the need for manual intervention, cutting down labor costs and increasing efficiency. Farmers can also optimize resource usage, which leads to cost savings.

- Example: **John Deere**, a leader in agricultural equipment, has integrated IoT technology into its machinery, allowing farmers to automate tasks like planting, fertilizing, and harvesting. This results in reduced labor costs and more efficient operations.

4. **Improved Decision-Making**
   - **Benefit:** The data collected by IoT devices allows farmers to make better decisions based on accurate, real-time insights into their operations, leading to more effective management of crops, livestock, and resources.
   - **Example: The Climate Corporation** offers digital agriculture solutions that use IoT sensors and data analytics to help farmers manage their fields. The system provides insights into weather patterns, soil health, and crop conditions, enabling farmers to make proactive, data-driven decisions.

5. **Sustainability and Environmental Impact**
   - **Benefit:** IoT technologies help promote sustainable farming practices by optimizing resource use, reducing waste, and minimizing the environmental footprint of agriculture.
   - **Example: Smart irrigation systems** powered by IoT and AI analyze soil moisture levels and

166

weather data to optimize water usage, ensuring crops receive sufficient irrigation while conserving water resources.

IoT is transforming agriculture by providing farmers with the tools to optimize their practices, increase yields, reduce costs, and improve sustainability. With the integration of sensors, drones, and automated systems, IoT is helping farmers make data-driven decisions that enhance both productivity and environmental stewardship.

CHAPTER 18

IOT IN RETAIL AND SUPPLY CHAIN

IoT Applications in Retail: Smart Shelves, Inventory Management

The retail sector has embraced IoT technology to enhance operational efficiency, improve customer experiences, and optimize inventory management. Through the use of connected devices and smart systems, IoT is transforming traditional retail operations, enabling retailers to offer more personalized services, streamline logistics, and reduce costs.

1. **Smart Shelves**

    o **Description:** Smart shelves are IoT-enabled shelving units that use sensors to detect stock levels in real-time. These shelves monitor product availability and alert store employees when an item needs to be restocked, preventing out-of-stock situations and improving the shopping experience.

    o **How It Works:** Smart shelves are equipped with weight sensors, RFID tags, or cameras that track product levels and send real-time data to a central system. This information can be accessed by store managers or employees via mobile apps or dashboard interfaces.

o **Benefits:**

- **Inventory Accuracy:** Retailers can track inventory more accurately, reducing the risk of stockouts and overstocking.

- **Improved Customer Experience:** Customers are more likely to find the products they need, which improves their satisfaction and loyalty.

- **Reduced Labor Costs:** Automated inventory tracking reduces the need for manual stocktaking, allowing employees to focus on other tasks.

2. IoT in Inventory Management

o **Description:** IoT-enabled inventory management systems use sensors, RFID tags, and GPS technology to provide real-time visibility into stock levels, location, and movement. This allows retailers to monitor inventory from warehouses to store shelves and improve supply chain efficiency.

o **How It Works:** RFID tags and sensors are placed on products or pallets to track their movement across the supply chain. These devices send data to cloud-based platforms, where inventory is

169

automatically updated and monitored in real-time.

- ○ **Benefits:**
  - ▪ **Real-Time Tracking:** Retailers can track inventory across multiple locations in real-time, ensuring they always have the right amount of stock.
  - ▪ **Supply Chain Optimization:** Real-time data helps streamline order fulfillment, reduce lead times, and ensure that products are replenished when needed.
  - ▪ **Cost Savings:** Automated inventory management reduces the cost of excess inventory and helps optimize stock levels to meet demand.

Tracking and Tracing Products with IoT

IoT enables product tracking and tracing at every stage of the supply chain, from production to delivery. Through RFID, GPS, and sensors, IoT offers enhanced visibility and control over the flow of goods, improving logistics efficiency, reducing theft, and ensuring compliance with safety regulations.

1. **Product Tracking with RFID and GPS**

   o **Description:** RFID (Radio Frequency Identification) and GPS (Global Positioning System) are used to track products as they move through the supply chain. Each item is tagged with an RFID chip or GPS sensor that transmits real-time data to a central system, allowing retailers and logistics providers to monitor product location and status.

   o **How It Works:** RFID tags or GPS sensors are attached to products, pallets, or containers. As products move through various stages of the supply chain, data about their location, condition (e.g., temperature, humidity), and status (e.g., in transit, in storage) is sent to cloud-based systems for analysis and tracking.

   o **Benefits:**

      ▪ **Improved Visibility:** Retailers can track products across the entire supply chain, ensuring timely deliveries and reducing inventory discrepancies.

      ▪ **Minimized Loss and Theft:** Real-time tracking makes it easier to detect and prevent theft or loss during transit.

      ▪ **Increased Efficiency:** IoT-based tracking helps automate the supply chain,

171

reducing the need for manual checks and optimizing logistics.

2. **Condition Monitoring During Transit**

   o **Description:** In industries where product quality is sensitive to conditions like temperature, humidity, or light exposure, IoT sensors are used to monitor environmental conditions during transit. This is particularly important in industries such as food, pharmaceuticals, and electronics.

   o **How It Works:** Sensors embedded in packaging or containers continuously monitor factors like temperature, humidity, and shock. If a product is exposed to conditions outside the acceptable range, alerts are sent to logistics managers to take corrective actions.

   o **Benefits:**

      ▪ **Product Quality Assurance:** Real-time monitoring ensures that products remain within required conditions, reducing the risk of spoilage or damage.

      ▪ **Compliance and Safety:** Many industries require products to meet specific environmental standards during transit. IoT ensures compliance with these regulations and prevents product recalls.

172

- **Reduced Waste:** By ensuring that products are stored and transported under the right conditions, businesses reduce waste and improve profitability.

Case Studies of IoT in Logistics and Supply Chain

IoT technologies are transforming logistics and supply chain operations by enabling real-time tracking, improving inventory management, and optimizing transportation routes. Below are some notable case studies that demonstrate the impact of IoT in logistics and supply chain management.

1. **Case Study 1: Walmart – IoT for Supply Chain Efficiency**
   - ○ **Scenario:** Walmart, one of the world's largest retailers, has incorporated IoT technologies into its supply chain management system to enhance operational efficiency and improve inventory management.
   - ○ **Solution:** Walmart uses IoT-enabled sensors and RFID technology to track products in real-time from suppliers to store shelves. This allows Walmart to monitor stock levels, optimize

173

replenishment schedules, and ensure products are available to customers without excess inventory.

- o **Outcome:** Walmart's use of IoT has resulted in better stock visibility, reduced out-of-stock situations, and improved order fulfillment accuracy. The system helps the company save costs by minimizing inventory waste and improving supply chain efficiency.

- o **Impact:** Enhanced customer satisfaction, improved supply chain agility, and significant cost reductions.

2. **Case Study 2: Maersk – IoT for Container Tracking**

- o **Scenario:** Maersk, a leading global shipping company, needed to optimize its container tracking and improve visibility into shipments across its global network.

- o **Solution:** Maersk implemented IoT sensors in shipping containers to track their location, condition (e.g., temperature), and movement. This data is transmitted in real-time to a centralized platform, enabling Maersk to provide customers with up-to-date information on their shipments.

- o **Outcome:** With IoT-based tracking, Maersk has improved container management and reduced

174

delays by ensuring timely delivery of goods. The system also helps monitor temperature-sensitive goods, such as pharmaceuticals and food, to ensure product quality.

- o **Impact:** Improved operational efficiency, reduced delays, and increased customer satisfaction with real-time visibility into shipments.

3. **Case Study 3: DHL – IoT for Smart Warehouses**

- o **Scenario:** DHL, a global logistics provider, wanted to improve warehouse operations by automating processes and increasing efficiency in order fulfillment.

- o **Solution:** DHL implemented IoT-enabled systems in its warehouses, including RFID tags to track inventory and robots to assist with picking and packing. IoT sensors monitor stock levels and automatically trigger reordering when inventory runs low.

- o **Outcome:** The IoT system has helped DHL optimize warehouse operations, reduce human error, and streamline order fulfillment. The use of automation and real-time inventory tracking has also improved warehouse efficiency and reduced labor costs.

- o **Impact:** Increased warehouse productivity, reduced operational costs, and faster, more accurate order fulfillment.

4. **Case Study 4: Amazon – IoT and Drones for Efficient Delivery**

    - o **Scenario:** Amazon wanted to optimize its delivery system and reduce the time it takes to fulfill orders for customers.

    - o **Solution:** Amazon uses IoT-enabled drones for last-mile delivery in certain areas. Drones equipped with GPS and IoT sensors can track their location, optimize delivery routes, and avoid obstacles in real-time. Additionally, Amazon uses IoT technology in its fulfillment centers to monitor inventory and coordinate drone dispatch.

    - o **Outcome:** By integrating IoT with drone technology, Amazon has reduced delivery times, improved logistics efficiency, and lowered costs associated with traditional delivery methods.

    - o **Impact:** Faster deliveries, improved customer satisfaction, and optimized logistics processes.

The integration of IoT in retail and supply chain management is driving operational efficiency, improving customer experiences, and reducing costs. Through the use of smart shelves, inventory management systems, real-time product tracking, and case studies from industry leaders like Walmart, Amazon, and Maersk, it's clear that IoT is transforming logistics and supply chains. These technologies enable more efficient operations, better decision-making, and greater visibility throughout the supply chain.

CHAPTER 19

BLOCKCHAIN AND IOT

Using Blockchain for IoT Security and Transparency

The combination of Blockchain and IoT holds significant promise for enhancing security, transparency, and trust in IoT networks. While IoT enables seamless communication between connected devices, it introduces several security concerns, such as unauthorized access, data breaches, and manipulation of information. Blockchain technology, with its decentralized and immutable nature, offers a powerful solution to address these challenges and ensure that IoT systems are more secure and transparent.

1. **Blockchain Basics for IoT Security**

    o **Decentralized Trust:** Blockchain operates as a distributed ledger where data is stored in multiple locations (nodes), making it extremely difficult for a single point of failure or a malicious actor to compromise the system. Each transaction (or data record) is linked to the previous one through cryptographic hashes, creating a chain of blocks that is nearly impossible to alter once recorded.

- o **Immutability and Transparency:** Each transaction added to the blockchain is time-stamped and verified by a network of participants. Once information is recorded on the blockchain, it cannot be changed, ensuring data integrity and transparency.

- o **Smart Contracts:** Blockchain-based smart contracts can automatically execute actions based on predefined conditions, reducing the need for intermediaries and enhancing automation and security in IoT environments.

2. **Blockchain's Role in Securing IoT Data**

- o **Data Integrity:** In an IoT network, devices continually generate data that can be sensitive or critical to business operations. Blockchain ensures that this data remains tamper-proof, as any attempt to alter the data would require changes to all subsequent blocks, which is computationally infeasible.

- o **Authentication and Authorization:** Blockchain can provide secure, decentralized methods for authenticating and authorizing IoT devices. This ensures that only authorized devices can access or exchange data within the network.

- o **Access Control:** Blockchain-based identity management systems allow for secure and controlled access to IoT devices and data. With blockchain, users and devices can have digital identities that are cryptographically verified, ensuring only legitimate participants are granted access.

How Blockchain Can Enable Secure Transactions in IoT Networks

In IoT networks, where devices communicate and exchange data autonomously, ensuring the security and privacy of transactions is critical. Blockchain offers a decentralized, secure way to facilitate these transactions, reducing reliance on centralized intermediaries and enabling peer-to-peer communication between IoT devices.

1. **Decentralized Peer-to-Peer Transactions**
   o **How It Works:** Blockchain allows IoT devices to securely interact with each other without the need for a central authority. For example, when two IoT devices need to exchange data or complete a transaction, the transaction can be verified and recorded on the blockchain, ensuring that it is secure, transparent, and traceable.
   o **Example:** In a smart home, different IoT devices (thermostats, lights, locks, etc.) can communicate

directly with each other using blockchain-based protocols. A smart contract could trigger the locking of doors once the home's security system is activated, or adjust the thermostat settings based on user preferences, all without needing an intermediary.

2. **Secure Payment and Microtransactions**

   o **How It Works:** Blockchain enables secure microtransactions between IoT devices by using cryptocurrencies or tokens. For example, IoT devices in a smart city could pay for services like data processing or power usage through small, automated transactions recorded on a blockchain.

   o **Example:** In a smart grid system, IoT-enabled devices can autonomously buy and sell energy between themselves using blockchain and cryptocurrency. For instance, a solar panel system could sell excess energy to the grid, and the transaction would be securely recorded on the blockchain, ensuring transparency and reducing fraud.

   o **Benefit:** This approach eliminates the need for a central intermediary (such as a utility company) and ensures that the transactions are secure, transparent, and trustworthy.

3. **Supply Chain and Logistics Management**

o **How It Works:** IoT devices in supply chains (e.g., sensors, RFID tags) can automatically track products, shipments, and inventory in real-time. Blockchain provides a secure and transparent ledger for recording these transactions, ensuring that all parties (manufacturers, distributors, retailers) can access the same immutable data.

o **Example:** In a pharmaceutical supply chain, each stage of the product's journey—manufacturing, shipping, and delivery—can be recorded on a blockchain. IoT sensors can track temperature, humidity, and location of the drugs, and blockchain ensures that all stakeholders (manufacturers, suppliers, regulators) can verify the authenticity and quality of the product at each step.

o **Benefit:** This improves transparency, reduces fraud, and ensures that only genuine products reach consumers.

Real-World Blockchain and IoT Integrations

Several industries have begun exploring and implementing blockchain and IoT integrations to improve security, streamline operations, and enhance transparency. Below are some real-world examples of how these technologies are being combined:

1. **Case Study 1: IBM Food Trust and Walmart**

   o **Overview:** IBM's Food Trust blockchain, in partnership with Walmart, leverages IoT sensors and blockchain technology to improve traceability and transparency in the food supply chain. Each step of the food journey—from farm to retail—is recorded on the blockchain, providing real-time tracking of products.

   o **How It Works:** IoT sensors monitor temperature, humidity, and other conditions of food products during transportation and storage. The data is recorded on a blockchain, which can be accessed by all participants in the supply chain, including farmers, manufacturers, and retailers.

   o **Outcome:** This integration helps prevent foodborne illness outbreaks by ensuring that contaminated products can be quickly traced to their source. It also improves supply chain efficiency by reducing waste and ensuring quality control.

○ **Impact:** Enhanced food safety, reduced waste, and increased transparency across the food supply chain.

2. **Case Study 2: VeChain and IoT for Supply Chain Transparency**

○ **Overview:** VeChain is a blockchain platform that uses IoT to enhance transparency in supply chains, particularly in luxury goods and pharmaceuticals. By combining IoT sensors with blockchain, VeChain provides consumers and businesses with real-time data on the authenticity and origin of products.

○ **How It Works:** IoT sensors are placed on products (such as luxury goods, pharmaceuticals, or wine) to track their location and condition during transportation. This data is recorded on the VeChain blockchain, ensuring transparency and enabling consumers to verify the authenticity of products.

○ **Outcome:** Consumers can scan QR codes to access product histories, confirming that the items they purchase are genuine. The blockchain also helps businesses optimize supply chain logistics by providing real-time data on the condition of products.

184

o **Impact:** Increased trust between consumers and businesses, reduced counterfeit goods, and enhanced product transparency.

3. **Case Study 3: Helium Network – IoT and Blockchain for Decentralized Wireless Networks**

   o **Overview:** The Helium Network is a decentralized wireless network for IoT devices that leverages blockchain to provide secure, low-cost connectivity. IoT devices use Helium's blockchain-based protocol to connect to a network of "hotspots," which are operated by individuals and businesses.

   o **How It Works:** Helium network participants deploy IoT devices (like sensors and trackers) and receive cryptocurrency-based rewards in exchange for providing network coverage. Blockchain ensures that all transactions, such as the transfer of IoT data and network usage, are secure and transparent.

   o **Outcome:** This integration creates a decentralized, scalable network for IoT devices, reducing the cost of connectivity and providing a secure environment for device communication.

   o **Impact:** Lower-cost IoT network infrastructure, increased scalability, and greater accessibility for IoT deployments worldwide.

185

4. **Case Study 4: IoTeX – Secure Data and Identity Management for IoT Devices**

- o **Overview:** IoTeX is a blockchain platform designed to secure IoT data and manage the identity of connected devices. By using blockchain, IoTeX ensures that IoT devices communicate securely and that data exchanged between devices is authenticated and encrypted.

- o **How It Works:** IoTeX creates a decentralized network of IoT devices that can verify and authenticate transactions using blockchain technology. This includes data exchange between devices such as smart thermostats, security cameras, and health devices.

- o **Outcome:** IoTeX provides a secure and transparent way for devices to share data without the need for centralized authorities, allowing for secure transactions and better privacy protection for users.

- o **Impact:** Enhanced privacy and security for IoT data, and more control for users over their connected devices.

Blockchain and IoT are working together to revolutionize a wide range of industries by improving security,

186

transparency, and operational efficiency. By providing decentralized, tamper-proof data storage and enabling secure transactions, blockchain enhances the trustworthiness of IoT networks and applications. Whether in supply chain management, food traceability, or secure IoT device interactions, the combination of blockchain and IoT is creating smarter, more reliable systems.

CHAPTER 20

DATA ANALYTICS IN IOT

The Importance of Data Analytics in IoT

The Internet of Things (IoT) generates vast amounts of data from sensors, devices, and systems deployed in various industries. Data analytics is crucial in IoT because it enables the conversion of raw data into valuable insights that can optimize processes, improve decision-making, and drive innovation. By analyzing IoT data effectively, businesses can improve operational efficiency, enhance customer experiences, reduce costs, and even predict future trends.

1. Turning Raw Data into Actionable Insights

- o **Explanation:** IoT devices generate continuous streams of data, often in real-time. Data analytics tools help to extract meaningful patterns and trends from this data, enabling organizations to make informed decisions. For instance, data from sensors on industrial machines can be analyzed to predict maintenance needs, reducing downtime and extending equipment lifespan.
- o **Benefits:**

188

- **Informed Decision Making:** Data analytics helps businesses understand the current state of their operations and make proactive decisions.
- **Predictive Maintenance:** By analyzing sensor data, businesses can predict equipment failures before they happen, improving reliability and reducing downtime.
- **Operational Optimization:** Data-driven insights can help organizations streamline their processes, improving efficiency and reducing waste.

2. **Enhanced Customer Experiences**

   o **Explanation:** In retail, healthcare, and other sectors, data analytics enables businesses to offer personalized services and experiences. For example, IoT sensors in smart homes can collect data on user preferences and habits, which can then be analyzed to automate actions such as adjusting the temperature or lighting based on the user's schedule.

   o **Benefits:**

   - **Personalized Services:** IoT data analytics allows businesses to offer customized services to customers, increasing satisfaction and loyalty.

- **Efficiency in Service Delivery:** By analyzing IoT data, businesses can identify pain points and optimize customer interactions.

3. **Automation and AI Integration**

   o **Explanation:** Analytics plays a key role in integrating AI with IoT, where AI models analyze data in real-time and make automated decisions without human intervention. For example, in a smart factory, IoT devices monitor the production line, and AI-powered data analytics can optimize workflows by automatically adjusting parameters such as speed and temperature.

   o **Benefits:**

     - **Operational Efficiency:** Real-time data analytics helps organizations automate tasks and workflows, improving overall efficiency.

     - **Faster Decision-Making:** Automation driven by data analytics allows for quicker decisions, reducing manual intervention and speeding up processes.

190

Real-Time vs. Batch Processing

When it comes to processing IoT data, organizations can choose between two main approaches: **real-time processing** and **batch processing**. Each has its use cases, benefits, and challenges, depending on the type of data and the requirements of the application.

1. **Real-Time Processing**
   o **Definition:** Real-time processing involves continuously analyzing data as it is generated, allowing for immediate action based on the insights gained. This is critical in applications where time-sensitive decisions are needed, such as autonomous vehicles, industrial automation, and health monitoring systems.
   o **How It Works:** Data is collected from IoT devices and transmitted to an analytics platform or edge device, where it is processed in real-time. The results are then used to trigger actions or alerts immediately.
   o **Benefits:**
      ▪ **Immediate Response:** Real-time analytics enable businesses to take immediate action based on the data, such

as adjusting machinery settings or sending alerts about potential issues.

- **Enhanced User Experience:** For applications like smart homes or personalized customer services, real-time processing ensures seamless and responsive experiences for users.

o **Examples:**

- **Smart Traffic Systems:** IoT sensors collect real-time data on traffic conditions, and AI-driven analytics process this data instantly to optimize traffic light timings and reduce congestion.

- **Wearable Health Devices:** IoT-enabled health monitors, such as fitness trackers and medical devices, process real-time data on heart rate, activity, and sleep patterns to provide instant feedback to users or healthcare providers.

2. **Batch Processing**

o **Definition:** Batch processing involves collecting and storing data over a period of time before processing it in large chunks, or "batches." This approach is suitable for use cases where real-time processing is not necessary, and data can be analyzed periodically.

- o **How It Works:** Data is gathered and stored in large datasets, typically over hours or days. Once the data has been accumulated, it is processed in bulk, and insights are generated in a periodic manner.
- o **Benefits:**
  - **Cost Efficiency:** Batch processing is typically more resource-efficient, as it doesn't require continuous processing and can take advantage of less frequent, high-volume analysis.
  - **Scalability:** It is well-suited for applications with large volumes of data where immediate action is not required, such as analyzing daily sales data or generating monthly reports.
- o **Examples:**
  - **Utility Consumption:** IoT sensors in smart meters collect data on water or energy consumption over the course of a day or week, and this data is processed in batches to generate monthly usage reports.

193

- **Inventory Management:** Retailers can process inventory data in batches at the end of the day to understand stock levels and generate reports for replenishment.

3. **Comparing Real-Time and Batch Processing**

   o **Real-Time Processing:** Suited for time-sensitive applications where immediate decisions are required (e.g., autonomous systems, healthcare monitoring, traffic control).

   o **Batch Processing:** Best for applications that can tolerate delays in data processing and require periodic updates, such as financial reporting, long-term trend analysis, and inventory tracking.

Tools and Platforms for IoT Data Analysis

There are a variety of tools and platforms available for analyzing the data generated by IoT devices. These platforms often combine data collection, processing, visualization, and reporting, enabling businesses to extract valuable insights from their IoT networks.

1. **IoT Platforms for Data Management**

   o **Amazon Web Services (AWS) IoT:** AWS IoT provides a suite of tools for managing and

194

analyzing data from IoT devices. It includes AWS IoT Core for device connectivity, AWS IoT Analytics for data analysis, and AWS IoT Greengrass for edge computing. AWS IoT Analytics allows businesses to filter, transform, and analyze data from multiple sources.

o **Microsoft Azure IoT:** Azure IoT provides a range of services for building IoT solutions, including data management and analytics tools. Azure IoT Hub allows for secure communication between IoT devices, while Azure IoT Central provides a platform for managing and analyzing IoT data.

o **Google Cloud IoT:** Google Cloud IoT integrates IoT data with powerful analytics tools like Google BigQuery and Google Cloud Machine Learning. These services allow businesses to process large datasets, analyze IoT data in real-time, and gain predictive insights using AI and ML.

o **IBM Watson IoT:** IBM's Watson IoT platform offers analytics, AI, and cognitive computing to analyze IoT data. It includes tools for visualizing data, detecting anomalies, and leveraging machine learning models to predict future trends.

2. **IoT Analytics Tools**

- o **Apache Kafka:** Kafka is an open-source platform for real-time data streaming and batch processing. It is widely used to manage large-scale IoT data streams and process data in real-time.

- o **Apache Spark:** Apache Spark is a fast, in-memory data processing engine that supports both real-time streaming and batch processing. It is used to process large datasets generated by IoT sensors and provide real-time insights.

- o **Node-RED:** Node-RED is a flow-based development tool for wiring together IoT devices, APIs, and online services. It's used to create applications that collect, analyze, and visualize IoT data.

3. **Data Visualization Tools**

- o **Tableau:** Tableau is a popular data visualization tool that integrates with IoT platforms to create interactive dashboards. It helps businesses visualize trends, patterns, and anomalies in IoT data.

- o **Power BI:** Microsoft Power BI provides similar functionality, allowing organizations to analyze and visualize IoT data from various sources, including cloud platforms and on-premise systems.

196

o **Grafana:** Grafana is an open-source platform for monitoring and analyzing IoT data. It integrates with various data sources, including databases and time-series data platforms, to create dashboards that display IoT metrics.

4. **Edge Computing and IoT Analytics**

o **EdgeX Foundry:** EdgeX Foundry is an open-source project that provides a common platform for edge computing in IoT. It helps businesses analyze IoT data at the edge, reducing the need for cloud processing and minimizing latency.

o **Fog Computing Platforms:** Fog computing platforms extend cloud capabilities to the edge of the network, providing real-time processing of IoT data close to the source. These platforms help reduce the volume of data sent to the cloud, enabling faster and more efficient decision-making.

Data analytics is at the core of IoT, enabling businesses to derive actionable insights from the vast amounts of data generated by connected devices. Real-time and batch processing serve different purposes depending on the requirements of the application, and there are numerous platforms and tools available to facilitate the analysis of IoT data. Whether using cloud platforms like AWS and Microsoft Azure, real-time processing tools like Apache Kafka, or edge computing solutions like EdgeX Foundry, businesses can leverage these technologies to optimize their IoT networks and gain valuable insights.

CHAPTER 21

BUILDING IOT SOLUTIONS: A STEP-BY-STEP GUIDE

Key Considerations in Designing an IoT Solution

Designing an IoT solution requires careful planning and attention to multiple factors to ensure the system is scalable, secure, and effective in solving the intended problem. The design process involves a combination of hardware, software, networking, and analytics components. Below are the critical considerations when designing an IoT solution:

1. **Defining the Problem and Objectives**
    - o **Description:** Before diving into the technical details, it's crucial to clearly define the problem the IoT solution is meant to solve and the objectives it needs to achieve. This includes understanding the end users' needs, the environment in which the solution will operate, and the desired outcomes (e.g., cost reduction, efficiency improvement, safety, etc.).
    - o **Example:** If the goal is to monitor and optimize energy consumption in a building, the problem definition should focus on energy efficiency,

199

real-time monitoring, and actionable insights for decision-makers.

2. **Choosing the Right IoT Devices and Sensors**

   o **Description:** Selecting the right sensors and devices is central to building an effective IoT solution. The choice of sensors depends on the data to be collected (e.g., temperature, humidity, motion, light) and the environment in which they will be deployed (e.g., industrial, agricultural, home). It's essential to ensure that the devices meet the required specifications in terms of accuracy, durability, and energy efficiency.

   o **Considerations:**

     ▪ **Power Requirements:** For battery-powered devices, it's crucial to choose sensors that are low power to extend battery life.

     ▪ **Connectivity:** The devices should support appropriate communication protocols like Wi-Fi, Zigbee, Bluetooth, or LPWAN, depending on the range and data transmission requirements.

     ▪ **Environmental Conditions:** Devices must be rugged enough to operate in harsh environments, such as extreme temperatures or humidity.

3. **Connectivity and Network Design**

- o **Description:** Connectivity is a critical component of any IoT solution. Deciding on the appropriate communication protocol (e.g., Wi-Fi, cellular, Bluetooth, LoRaWAN) depends on factors like data transmission range, power consumption, and network coverage.

- o **Considerations:**

  - **Data Volume and Speed:** For applications requiring high-speed data transmission, Wi-Fi or cellular might be preferred. For low-bandwidth and long-range applications (e.g., in remote areas), LPWAN or Zigbee might be more suitable.

  - **Network Scalability:** Ensure the network can handle the expected number of devices and be easily scaled as more devices are added over time.

  - **Security:** Secure communication protocols (e.g., TLS, SSL) should be used to protect the integrity and confidentiality of the data.

4. **Data Management and Analytics**

- o **Description:** Once IoT devices collect data, it must be processed, analyzed, and used to drive

201

meaningful insights. This involves choosing the right platforms for data storage, data processing (edge or cloud computing), and analytics tools for real-time or batch processing.

- o **Considerations:**
  - • **Data Storage:** Decide whether the data should be stored locally (on-device or on-edge servers) or in the cloud, based on factors such as latency, bandwidth, and security.
  - • **Data Analysis:** Implement data analytics tools to make sense of the collected data. This could involve simple data aggregation or advanced machine learning models for predictive analytics.
  - • **Real-Time vs. Batch Processing:** Based on the use case, decide whether real-time data processing is required (e.g., in critical systems like healthcare) or if batch processing will suffice (e.g., in some industrial monitoring systems).

5. **Security and Privacy**
   - o **Description:** Security is one of the top priorities in IoT solution design. Since IoT devices are often connected to the internet, they become vulnerable to cyberattacks and data breaches.

Implementing robust security measures for both devices and data is essential to protect the integrity and privacy of the system.

- o **Considerations:**
  - • **Authentication and Authorization:** Use secure protocols for device authentication and access control to ensure that only authorized devices and users can access the system.
  - • **Data Encryption:** Encrypt data both in transit (over networks) and at rest (in databases) to prevent unauthorized access or tampering.
  - • **Firmware and Software Updates:** Ensure that devices can be securely updated to patch vulnerabilities and add new features.

6. **Scalability and Future-Proofing**
   - o **Description:** As the number of IoT devices grows, so does the complexity of managing them. Design your IoT solution with scalability in mind so that it can handle increased device load and data volume in the future. Additionally, ensure that the solution is adaptable to future technologies and standards.
   - o **Considerations:**

- **Modular Design:** Build a solution that can easily be expanded or modified to incorporate new devices, sensors, or analytics tools.
- **Interoperability:** Ensure the solution supports industry standards and can integrate with other systems or platforms, allowing for future enhancements or expansions.

Hardware and Software Integration

The success of an IoT solution relies on seamless integration between the hardware (sensors, devices, actuators) and software (platforms, applications, analytics). Here's how hardware and software can be integrated:

1. **Hardware Integration**
   - **Sensors and Actuators:** The physical devices used to collect data (sensors) and perform actions (actuators) form the foundation of the IoT system. These devices must be integrated with the software that collects, processes, and acts on the data they generate.
   - **Microcontrollers and Edge Devices:** IoT devices often rely on microcontrollers (e.g.,

Raspberry Pi, Arduino) to process data locally before transmitting it to the cloud. Edge devices can preprocess data, reducing the load on cloud servers and minimizing latency for time-sensitive applications.

o **Connectivity Modules:** Modules like Wi-Fi, Bluetooth, Zigbee, or LoRaWAN are used to enable communication between IoT devices and the central network. These modules must be chosen based on range, power consumption, and data throughput needs.

2. **Software Integration**

o **IoT Platforms:** Software platforms such as AWS IoT, Google Cloud IoT, or Microsoft Azure IoT Hub provide cloud infrastructure for managing devices, processing data, and performing analytics. These platforms offer pre-built APIs and SDKs that enable easy integration with various IoT devices and sensors.

o **Edge Computing:** For real-time applications, edge computing platforms like EdgeX Foundry or Azure IoT Edge allow data to be processed at the device or edge level, reducing latency and network traffic. Edge computing is critical in environments where real-time decisions are

205

required, such as autonomous vehicles or industrial automation.

- o **Data Analytics and Visualization:** IoT data must be processed and analyzed. Platforms like Apache Kafka (for data streaming), Apache Spark (for big data analytics), and Tableau (for data visualization) help turn raw IoT data into actionable insights.

Real-World Example of Building an IoT System

Let's take a practical example of building an IoT system for **smart farming**, which monitors soil moisture and adjusts irrigation accordingly.

1. **Step 1: Defining the Problem**
   - o The goal is to optimize water usage for irrigation by monitoring soil moisture levels in real-time and adjusting watering schedules based on actual conditions.

2. **Step 2: Selecting the Right Devices**
   - o **Sensors:** Soil moisture sensors are placed in the ground to monitor moisture levels.
   - o **Actuators:** Solenoid valves control water flow into the irrigation system, which will be automated based on the sensor data.

206

3. **Step 3: Connectivity**

   o The sensors and actuators are connected to a central hub via **LoRaWAN** (Low Power Wide Area Network) to handle long-range communication with minimal power consumption.

4. **Step 4: Data Collection and Processing**

   o The sensor data is sent to an IoT platform like **AWS IoT Core**, where it is collected, processed, and stored. The data is then analyzed to determine the soil's water requirements.

5. **Step 5: Automation and Control**

   o **Automation Logic:** Based on the soil moisture readings, a smart contract or automated rule is triggered to open or close the solenoid valve. If the soil moisture is too low, the system will activate irrigation to provide the necessary water.

6. **Step 6: Data Analytics**

   o Data from multiple fields can be analyzed over time to identify patterns in water usage, allowing farmers to optimize irrigation schedules based on seasonal trends.

7. **Step 7: Security**

   o The system is secured with device authentication using **TLS encryption** for data transmission and **OAuth2** for user authentication to ensure only authorized personnel can control the irrigation system.

8. **Step 8: Scalability**

   o   As the farm grows, additional sensors and actuators can be added to the system. The IoT platform can scale to manage more devices and handle larger volumes of data.

Building an IoT solution requires a comprehensive approach that spans from problem definition to hardware/software integration, real-time processing, and security considerations. By following a step-by-step process, you can design, implement, and scale a solution that meets the needs of your specific application.

CHAPTER 22

SCALABILITY AND PERFORMANCE IN IOT

Challenges of Scaling IoT Systems

As IoT systems grow and more devices are added to a network, ensuring scalability and performance optimization becomes increasingly difficult. Scaling IoT systems involves not only managing the larger volume of devices and data but also ensuring that the infrastructure can handle the additional load while maintaining speed, security, and reliability.

1. **Managing Large Volumes of Data**
   - o **Challenge:** One of the most significant challenges of scaling IoT systems is handling the vast amounts of data generated by an increasing number of connected devices. The more devices you have, the more data is produced, and this data must be efficiently processed, stored, and analyzed without overwhelming the system.
   - o **Solution:** Implement edge computing to process data locally on devices or edge nodes, reducing the volume of data that needs to be sent to the

cloud. This helps to alleviate network congestion and minimizes latency for real-time applications.

2. **Device and Network Management**

   o **Challenge:** As the number of devices in an IoT network increases, managing their connectivity, configuration, and firmware updates becomes more complex. In a large-scale system, keeping track of devices, ensuring they are properly configured, and ensuring seamless communication can be a daunting task.

   o **Solution:** Use IoT management platforms that offer device lifecycle management, centralized monitoring, and secure over-the-air (OTA) firmware updates. These platforms help streamline device management and provide a unified view of all devices in the network.

3. **Network Congestion and Bandwidth Limitations**

   o **Challenge:** Scaling IoT systems requires robust and efficient communication networks. As more devices are added, the network must support higher traffic volumes and longer distances while ensuring low latency. Bandwidth limitations can become a bottleneck, particularly for applications requiring real-time data.

   o **Solution:** Leverage low-power wide-area networks (LPWAN) or 5G connectivity, which are designed to support large numbers of IoT devices and can efficiently handle massive amounts of data. Additionally, using protocols like MQTT or CoAP for lightweight messaging can reduce the overhead of data transmission.

4. **Ensuring Security at Scale**

   o **Challenge:** With more devices and data in an IoT system, security becomes a major concern. Protecting data integrity, ensuring secure device authentication, and preventing unauthorized access are crucial for large-scale deployments.

   o **Solution:** Implement robust security measures such as end-to-end encryption, secure device authentication, and role-based access control (RBAC). Blockchain can also be used to ensure secure transactions and data integrity, especially in large-scale IoT networks where trust and transparency are critical.

5. **Cost Management**

   o **Challenge:** As IoT systems scale, the costs of maintaining and expanding infrastructure can grow exponentially. From hardware to cloud storage and processing, scaling IoT systems can become costly, particularly in the case of large-scale deployments.

- ○ **Solution:** Optimize infrastructure by using cloud-based services that offer scalability and pay-as-you-go pricing models. Additionally, using edge computing can reduce the need for extensive cloud resources, helping to manage costs by processing data closer to the source.

Best Practices for Performance Optimization

To ensure that IoT systems perform optimally as they scale, it is essential to follow certain best practices. These practices help balance the load across devices, networks, and servers while maintaining a high level of performance and minimizing downtime.

1. **Edge Computing for Reduced Latency**
   - ○ **Explanation:** By processing data closer to the source (on the edge), IoT systems can reduce the amount of data that needs to be sent to the cloud. This reduces latency, enhances real-time decision-making, and minimizes bandwidth usage.
   - ○ **Best Practice:** Deploy edge devices to filter, preprocess, and analyze data locally before sending it to the cloud. For example, in a smart

212

factory, sensors can process data about machine conditions locally and only send alerts or anomalies to the cloud for further analysis.

2. Load Balancing Across the Network

- o **Explanation:** Load balancing helps distribute the incoming traffic evenly across multiple servers, preventing any single server from being overloaded. This ensures that the system remains responsive and efficient even as the number of devices increases.

- o **Best Practice:** Use load balancers to distribute traffic between edge nodes, gateways, and cloud servers. This helps to ensure that each component of the system is optimally utilized and prevents performance bottlenecks.

3. Data Compression and Filtering

- o **Explanation:** Sending raw data from IoT devices to the cloud can result in high bandwidth consumption. Data compression and filtering techniques reduce the volume of data being transmitted without losing critical information, improving overall performance.

- o **Best Practice:** Implement data filtering at the edge or on the devices to only transmit meaningful or actionable data. Use compression algorithms to reduce the size of the data packets

213

sent to the cloud, ensuring more efficient data transmission.

4. **Scalable Cloud Infrastructure**

   o **Explanation:** Cloud services offer on-demand resources that can be easily scaled up or down based on demand. Choosing a scalable cloud infrastructure is crucial for handling the growing needs of IoT systems.

   o **Best Practice:** Use cloud platforms like AWS IoT, Microsoft Azure, or Google Cloud IoT, which provide auto-scaling features that dynamically adjust resources based on incoming data volume and processing needs.

5. **Optimizing Power Consumption**

   o **Explanation:** Many IoT devices, especially those deployed in remote or outdoor environments, run on battery power. Optimizing power consumption ensures that devices have a longer lifespan and reduces the need for frequent maintenance.

   o **Best Practice:** Implement power-saving modes in IoT devices. Use low-power communication protocols (e.g., LoRaWAN or Zigbee) and ensure devices go into sleep mode when not in use. Solar-powered IoT systems are also becoming more popular for remote, off-grid deployments.

214

6. **Regular Monitoring and Maintenance**

   o **Explanation:** Continuous monitoring of the IoT network helps detect performance issues and potential failures early. Regular maintenance ensures that devices are functioning properly and up-to-date with the latest firmware and software.

   o **Best Practice:** Use IoT management platforms that provide real-time monitoring, automated diagnostics, and alerts for performance issues. Schedule routine updates and maintenance to ensure devices are always operating at peak efficiency.

Real-World Examples of Scalable IoT Solutions

Several industries have successfully implemented scalable IoT systems that have allowed them to grow and adapt to increasing demands. Below are examples of how scalability and performance optimization have been applied in real-world IoT solutions:

1. **Case Study 1: Smart Agriculture in Precision Farming**

   o **Scenario:** A large-scale farm needed a way to monitor soil moisture, weather conditions, and crop health across hundreds of acres. They wanted a solution that could scale as they expanded operations while ensuring real-time data analysis for better irrigation and fertilization.

o **Solution:** The farm deployed a combination of IoT sensors (soil moisture sensors, weather stations, drones) and edge computing devices to process data locally. The system is connected to the cloud to analyze long-term trends and provide predictive insights.

o **Outcome:** The system scaled easily by adding more sensors as the farm expanded. By processing data at the edge, latency was reduced, and bandwidth usage was optimized. The farm saw improved crop yields, reduced water usage, and optimized fertilizer application.

o **Impact:** Scalable solution that reduced costs and increased efficiency, allowing the farm to grow without significant performance degradation.

2. **Case Study 2: Smart City Infrastructure**

o **Scenario:** A city implemented a smart traffic management system using IoT sensors to monitor traffic flow and reduce congestion. The system needed to scale as the city expanded its urban infrastructure and population.

o **Solution:** The city implemented a cloud-based IoT platform that supported auto-scaling for real-time traffic monitoring. Smart traffic lights were controlled by IoT sensors, which adjusted timing based on traffic flow data. The system could handle data from thousands of sensors across the city.

o **Outcome:** The traffic management system improved traffic flow, reduced congestion, and cut down on pollution. The system was easily scaled to accommodate new roads and intersections as the city grew.

o **Impact:** The smart traffic solution provided a scalable infrastructure that improved city management, reduced traffic-related problems, and enhanced the overall quality of urban life.

3. **Case Study 3: Industrial IoT (IIoT) for Predictive Maintenance**

o **Scenario:** A manufacturing plant wanted to implement a predictive maintenance system to monitor the health of equipment and reduce downtime due to unexpected failures. The system needed to scale across multiple production lines and plants.

o **Solution:** The plant installed IoT sensors on critical equipment to monitor factors like temperature, vibration, and pressure. Data was processed in real-time at the edge, with alerts sent to maintenance teams for immediate action. The system was integrated with a cloud platform for analytics and long-term trend analysis.

○ **Outcome:** The predictive maintenance system reduced downtime by 30% and extended equipment lifespan. The solution was easily scaled to include additional machines as the plant expanded.

○ **Impact:** Increased operational efficiency, reduced maintenance costs, and enhanced equipment reliability.

Scaling IoT systems requires a strategic approach to managing data, optimizing performance, and ensuring the system can handle growing demands. By using best practices such as edge computing, load balancing, and scalable cloud infrastructure, businesses can ensure that their IoT solutions are both scalable and performant. Real-world examples from agriculture, smart cities, and industrial IoT show how scalable solutions can drive efficiency, reduce costs, and support growth.

CHAPTER 23

MANAGING IOT DEPLOYMENTS

End-to-End Deployment Strategies for IoT Systems

Successfully deploying an IoT system involves a series of strategic steps that cover everything from initial planning to post-deployment maintenance. An end-to-end deployment strategy ensures that all components of the IoT solution, including hardware, software, and network infrastructure, work seamlessly together to meet the business objectives.

1. **Planning and Requirements Gathering**

   o **Description:** Before starting the deployment, it's crucial to clearly define the objectives and requirements of the IoT system. This includes understanding the problem you're solving, the desired outcomes, the devices and sensors needed, and how data will be processed and utilized.

   o **Steps:**

     ▪ **Identify the Problem:** Understand the pain points and determine how IoT can solve the issue. This may involve reducing energy consumption,

219

improving efficiency, or enhancing customer experience.

- **Define KPIs:** Set clear Key Performance Indicators (KPIs) to measure the success of the IoT deployment. For example, in a smart building deployment, KPIs could include energy savings, system uptime, and user satisfaction.

- **Infrastructure Assessment:** Evaluate existing infrastructure to ensure compatibility with IoT devices and identify any potential gaps in network coverage, storage, or processing power.

2. **Device Selection and Integration**

- ○ **Description:** Choosing the right IoT devices, sensors, and actuators is essential for meeting system requirements. These devices must be compatible with the communication protocols (e.g., Wi-Fi, Bluetooth, Zigbee) and the desired data processing architecture (cloud or edge).

- ○ **Steps:**

  - **Sensor and Device Selection:** Choose sensors based on the data needed (e.g., temperature, humidity, motion) and ensure they meet accuracy and durability requirements.

220

- **Connectivity Solutions:** Decide on communication protocols (e.g., Wi-Fi, cellular, LPWAN) based on range, bandwidth, and energy consumption needs. For remote deployments, low-power networks like LoRaWAN may be ideal, while high-bandwidth applications may require Wi-Fi or 5G.
- **Integration:** Ensure that devices and sensors are compatible with the software platforms used for data processing and analytics. Platforms like AWS IoT, Google Cloud IoT, or Microsoft Azure provide pre-built connectors to facilitate integration.

3. **Network Design and Connectivity Setup**
   - o **Description:** IoT networks must be designed to handle the specific needs of the deployment, including device connectivity, data throughput, and security. This involves selecting the right network infrastructure, ensuring adequate coverage, and minimizing data transmission delays.
   - o **Steps:**
     - **Connectivity Setup:** Configure network infrastructure to ensure reliable

221

connectivity across the IoT devices. This includes setting up local networks (e.g., Wi-Fi, Zigbee) or long-range networks (e.g., LPWAN, cellular).

- **Edge and Cloud Integration:** Determine if edge computing is required for real-time data processing. If so, deploy edge nodes or gateways to preprocess data locally before sending it to the cloud for storage and further analysis.

4. **Deployment and Installation**

   o **Description:** Physical installation of IoT devices is a critical step in ensuring that the system operates as intended. Devices must be placed strategically to ensure full coverage and accurate data collection, and the deployment process should minimize disruptions to existing operations.

   o **Steps:**

      - **Device Installation:** Ensure that devices are placed in optimal locations, taking into account environmental factors (e.g., exposure to weather, interference) and their connectivity to the network.

- **Configuration and Testing:** After installation, configure devices with necessary software, connect them to the network, and conduct initial testing to verify their functionality.

- **System Integration:** Ensure that all devices are connected to the central platform and that data flows smoothly between sensors, gateways, and cloud systems.

5. **Monitoring and Maintenance**

   o **Description:** After deployment, continuous monitoring is essential to ensure the system functions as intended and meets performance goals. Additionally, regular maintenance, including firmware updates, device health checks, and data integrity audits, is necessary to maintain system reliability.

   o **Steps:**

     - **Real-Time Monitoring:** Use IoT management platforms to monitor device status, connectivity, and data flow. Implement automated alerts to notify the team of any system anomalies.

     - **Firmware and Software Updates:** Regularly update devices with new

223

firmware to fix bugs, enhance security, and add new features.

- **Scalability Planning:** As the system scales, ensure that additional devices, sensors, and infrastructure can be seamlessly integrated without compromising performance.

Testing and Troubleshooting IoT Deployments

Testing and troubleshooting are crucial to ensure that IoT systems operate as expected and deliver reliable performance. Effective testing verifies that all components of the system—devices, connectivity, platforms—work together cohesively and meet the desired objectives.

1. **Pre-Deployment Testing**
   o **Device Functionality Testing:** Before installation, thoroughly test the sensors and devices to ensure they function as expected. This includes verifying their range, sensitivity, battery life, and data transmission capabilities.
   o **Connectivity Testing:** Test communication between IoT devices, gateways, and the cloud to ensure reliable data transmission. Verify that all

devices are properly configured to communicate via the chosen network protocols.

- o **Integration Testing:** Ensure that devices integrate correctly with the cloud platform or edge computing infrastructure. This involves verifying that data is being transmitted, processed, and stored accurately.

2. Post-Deployment Troubleshooting

- o **Monitoring Data Flow:** After deployment, use real-time monitoring tools to check the flow of data from devices to the cloud. Ensure there are no disruptions in data transmission and that data is being processed in the desired time frame.

- o **Connectivity Issues:** If devices experience connectivity issues, troubleshoot network configurations, check signal strength, and verify that network infrastructure supports the growing number of devices.

- o **Device Malfunctions:** Troubleshoot individual devices for issues such as battery failure, hardware malfunctions, or sensor calibration errors. Regular diagnostics can help identify and resolve issues early.

3. Performance Testing

- o **Stress Testing:** Simulate high-load conditions to test the performance and scalability of the system.

225

Ensure that the system can handle the expected number of devices and data throughput without degrading performance.

- o **Latency and Response Time:** For real-time applications (e.g., autonomous vehicles, industrial automation), test the system's response time to ensure it meets the required latency thresholds.

4. **Security Testing**

- o **Vulnerability Assessment:** Regularly test IoT devices and networks for vulnerabilities, such as weak authentication, unencrypted communication, and exposed endpoints. Penetration testing can help identify security gaps.

- o **Encryption and Access Control:** Ensure that data encryption, secure device authentication, and proper access control measures are implemented and functioning correctly.

Case Study of an IoT System Rollout

To understand how to manage an IoT deployment, let's examine a case study of an IoT rollout for a **smart**

agricultural irrigation system that uses soil moisture sensors to optimize water usage on a large farm.

1. **Problem Definition:**
   o The goal was to optimize water usage on the farm by implementing an IoT-based irrigation system that monitors soil moisture levels in real time and automatically adjusts irrigation schedules.

2. **Planning and Device Selection:**
   o The farm team identified the need for soil moisture sensors, actuators to control water flow, and a cloud platform to monitor and manage the system. They selected LoRaWAN as the communication protocol for its low-power, long-range capabilities.
   o They defined KPIs such as water consumption reduction and system uptime.

3. **Connectivity Setup and Installation:**
   o The IoT devices were installed in key areas of the farm where moisture levels were critical. Sensors were placed in the soil at varying depths across the fields.
   o LoRaWAN gateways were installed to ensure full coverage of the farm, providing reliable communication between the sensors and the cloud platform.

- o Initial testing was conducted to verify that the sensors were transmitting accurate data and that the irrigation system was triggered when necessary.

4. **Integration with Cloud Platform:**
   - o The system was integrated with a cloud-based IoT platform for real-time monitoring. The platform was configured to send alerts when soil moisture levels fell below the predefined threshold, triggering automated irrigation.
   - o Data from the sensors was collected and stored for analysis, allowing the farm team to identify trends and further optimize irrigation schedules.

5. **Monitoring and Maintenance:**
   - o After deployment, the farm team used the IoT management platform to monitor system performance and device health. Regular checks were scheduled to ensure that the sensors remained calibrated, and the system continued to meet water usage reduction targets.
   - o The farm system was scaled to include additional sensors and irrigation zones as required.

6. **Outcome:**
   - o The IoT-based irrigation system successfully reduced water consumption by 30%, providing

significant cost savings and contributing to more sustainable farming practices.

o   The system scaled effectively, and the farm was able to add more sensors without significant changes to the infrastructure.

Managing IoT deployments requires careful planning, testing, and ongoing maintenance to ensure that the system delivers the expected results. From device selection and network setup to troubleshooting and performance testing, the deployment process must be carefully orchestrated to ensure reliability, security, and scalability.

CHAPTER 24

FUTURE TRENDS IN IOT

The Future of IoT: 5G, AI, and Beyond

The Internet of Things (IoT) has already transformed various industries, but the future promises even more significant advancements. As new technologies like 5G and AI continue to evolve, they will further unlock the potential of IoT, enabling new use cases, improving performance, and enhancing the integration of IoT systems with other digital technologies.

1. **5G and Its Impact on IoT**
   - **Overview:** 5G technology is expected to revolutionize IoT by providing ultra-fast data speeds, low latency, and higher bandwidth, which are essential for supporting large-scale IoT deployments. With 5G, IoT devices will be able to communicate more efficiently and in real-time, enabling a range of new applications in areas such as autonomous vehicles, remote healthcare, and smart cities.
   - **Benefits for IoT:**

- **Faster Speeds:** 5G's high-speed data transfer will allow IoT devices to exchange data much more quickly, making real-time applications like autonomous driving and industrial automation more effective.

- **Low Latency:** With ultra-low latency, 5G will enable instant communication between devices, reducing delays and improving the responsiveness of IoT systems.

- **Massive Device Connectivity:** 5G can support a far greater number of IoT devices in dense environments, such as smart cities or industrial settings, providing reliable connections for millions of devices.

- **Improved Mobile IoT:** 5G will enhance IoT solutions that require mobility, such as wearable health devices or connected vehicles, by offering stable and high-speed connectivity.

2. **AI and Machine Learning in IoT**

   o **Overview:** AI and machine learning (ML) will continue to play a pivotal role in IoT. As IoT devices generate more data, AI algorithms will become essential in processing and analyzing this information to provide actionable insights, predict outcomes, and automate decision-making.

- o **AI-Driven Analytics:** AI-powered analytics can help make sense of the vast amounts of data IoT devices collect. Through techniques like pattern recognition and anomaly detection, AI can uncover hidden trends, predict future behaviors, and optimize IoT system performance.

- o **Automation and Predictive Maintenance:** AI will automate tasks based on data from IoT devices, such as adjusting energy usage in buildings, managing traffic in smart cities, and performing predictive maintenance in industrial operations. This will reduce human intervention, lower costs, and improve operational efficiency.

- o **Personalization:** In consumer IoT applications, AI can help provide personalized experiences by analyzing user data and tailoring recommendations. Smart home systems, for instance, will learn users' habits and preferences and adjust home environments accordingly.

3. **Blockchain and IoT**

- o **Overview:** Blockchain technology, known for its decentralization and security, will become increasingly important for IoT applications. By ensuring data integrity, authenticity, and transparency, blockchain will address IoT's inherent security and privacy concerns.

- o **Benefits for IoT:**
  - ▪ **Secure Data Transactions:** Blockchain will ensure that IoT devices can exchange data securely, preventing unauthorized access and tampering.
  - ▪ **Decentralized IoT Networks:** Blockchain can support the creation of decentralized IoT networks, reducing dependency on central authorities and improving scalability.
  - ▪ **Smart Contracts:** Blockchain-based smart contracts can automate transactions and processes in IoT networks, enabling devices to make autonomous decisions.

Emerging Technologies and Their Impact on IoT

The convergence of IoT with several emerging technologies will drive innovation across industries and unlock new possibilities. These technologies, including edge computing,

233

augmented reality (AR), and quantum computing, will reshape the way IoT systems are designed and used.

1. **Edge Computing and IoT**

    o **Overview:** Edge computing involves processing data closer to the source (on the edge of the network) rather than relying on centralized cloud servers. This is particularly important for IoT systems where low latency, high-speed processing, and bandwidth efficiency are critical.

    o **Impact on IoT:**

        ▪ **Real-Time Data Processing:** With edge computing, IoT devices can process data locally, reducing latency and enabling real-time decision-making in applications like autonomous vehicles or industrial robotics.

        ▪ **Bandwidth Optimization:** By filtering and analyzing data at the edge, only relevant data is sent to the cloud, reducing bandwidth consumption and optimizing network performance.

        ▪ **Resilience and Reliability:** Edge computing can improve the reliability of IoT systems by enabling devices to

234

function autonomously, even when disconnected from the cloud.

2. **Augmented Reality (AR) and IoT**

o **Overview:** The combination of AR and IoT will enable interactive and immersive experiences for users, particularly in industries like retail, healthcare, and manufacturing. By overlaying digital information onto the physical world, AR can enhance the value of IoT data.

o **Impact on IoT:**

▪ **Interactive Interfaces:** In retail, IoT devices can transmit data to AR-enabled devices, providing customers with interactive product information. In manufacturing, AR glasses can display real-time data from IoT sensors, helping workers with tasks such as machine maintenance or assembly.

▪ **Training and Assistance:** AR can provide training for workers by guiding them through tasks with step-by-step visual instructions, based on data from IoT sensors or cameras.

▪ **Remote Assistance:** IoT sensors can enable real-time remote assistance through AR, allowing experts to diagnose problems or guide users in troubleshooting devices.

3. **Quantum Computing and IoT**

- o **Overview:** While still in its early stages, quantum computing has the potential to revolutionize IoT by enabling faster processing and solving complex problems that are currently out of reach for classical computers.

- o **Impact on IoT:**

  - **Advanced Data Analysis:** Quantum computing could dramatically speed up data analysis, enabling faster decision-making and more accurate predictions for IoT systems, particularly in industries like healthcare, finance, and logistics.

  - **Optimization:** Quantum algorithms could be used to optimize large-scale IoT networks, improving performance, energy efficiency, and resource allocation across connected devices.

  - **Security:** Quantum cryptography could provide more robust security measures for IoT networks, ensuring that data remains protected against future threats.

Predictions for the Next Decade

As IoT technology continues to evolve, we can expect significant advancements in the next decade that will reshape industries and create new opportunities. Below are some predictions for how IoT will develop over the next ten years:

1. **Ubiquitous IoT Integration**
   - **Prediction:** IoT devices will become increasingly integrated into every aspect of daily life, from homes and cities to healthcare, agriculture, and manufacturing. By 2030, it's predicted that there will be **over 50 billion connected devices** globally, creating an interconnected world of sensors, machines, and devices.
   - **Impact:** IoT will enhance the functionality of everyday objects, making them smarter, more efficient, and capable of communicating with other devices autonomously.

2. **AI-Driven IoT Systems**
   - **Prediction:** AI will play a more prominent role in managing and analyzing IoT systems. In the next decade, AI algorithms will become more capable of handling complex IoT data, allowing for self-learning systems that adapt to changing

237

conditions and optimize performance in real-time.

- o **Impact:** We will see more autonomous IoT systems that don't require human intervention to make decisions. For example, smart homes will automatically adjust environments based on user preferences, while industrial systems will anticipate maintenance needs without requiring manual checks.

3. **IoT in Healthcare**

- o **Prediction:** IoT will revolutionize healthcare by providing real-time health monitoring and enabling remote diagnosis and treatment. Wearable IoT devices will track vital signs and predict health issues before they become critical.

- o **Impact:** The healthcare industry will shift towards preventative care, reducing hospital visits and improving patient outcomes through continuous monitoring.

4. **Smart Cities and Infrastructure**

- o **Prediction:** Smart city deployments will increase, with IoT systems managing everything from traffic to waste disposal, energy consumption, and public services. By 2030, many cities will be fully integrated with IoT

238

technologies, improving sustainability and quality of life.

- o **Impact:** Smart cities will become more efficient, reducing congestion, improving safety, and enhancing the delivery of public services through IoT-connected infrastructure.

5. **5G and IoT Convergence**

- o **Prediction:** The rollout of 5G will fuel the growth of IoT by providing the necessary high-speed, low-latency connectivity to support large-scale IoT deployments. By the end of the decade, we will see highly reliable and fast networks that can support millions of connected devices in real-time.
- o **Impact:** 5G will enable next-generation IoT applications such as autonomous vehicles, smart cities, and real-time industrial monitoring, with seamless and instantaneous data transfer between devices.

The next decade promises exciting advancements in IoT, fueled by technologies like 5G, AI, edge computing, and blockchain. These innovations will transform industries, enhance user experiences, and create new business opportunities. As IoT continues to evolve, it will become an integral part of our daily lives, from improving health and efficiency to optimizing cities and industries.

CHAPTER 25

ETHICAL AND LEGAL CONSIDERATIONS IN IOT

IoT Privacy and Data Protection Concerns

The rapid growth of IoT devices has raised significant privacy and data protection concerns. IoT systems often collect vast amounts of sensitive data about individuals, homes, businesses, and environments. This data, if not handled properly, can lead to serious breaches of privacy, unauthorized access, and misuse. Therefore, understanding the privacy implications and ensuring robust data protection are critical in IoT system design and deployment.

1. **Types of Data Collected by IoT Devices**
    o **Personal Data:** Many IoT devices collect personal data such as location, health status, and usage patterns. For instance, smart home devices track users' schedules, while wearable health devices monitor vital signs.
    o **Environmental Data:** Sensors used in smart cities, agriculture, and industrial IoT systems collect data on temperature, humidity, and air

241

quality. While this data is useful for optimizing operations, it may also contain insights into personal behaviors and habits.

o **Data from Embedded Sensors:** Devices like security cameras and voice assistants capture personal or private information, which can lead to concerns about surveillance and misuse.

2. Privacy Risks in IoT Systems

o **Unauthorized Data Access:** IoT devices often send data to cloud platforms, creating a potential risk of unauthorized access or hacking. If the cloud infrastructure or communication protocols are not secure, attackers can intercept sensitive data.

o **Data Misuse:** Data collected from IoT devices can be sold or shared with third parties without proper consent from users, leading to privacy violations and exploitation.

o **Surveillance Concerns:** Devices like smart cameras and voice assistants raise concerns about constant surveillance, especially in homes and public spaces.

3. Ensuring Privacy and Data Protection

o **Encryption:** Data transmitted between IoT devices and cloud servers should be encrypted to prevent interception and unauthorized access.

242

End-to-end encryption ensures that only authorized parties can read the data.

- o **User Consent and Transparency:** IoT companies must obtain explicit consent from users before collecting personal data. Users should be fully informed about what data is being collected, how it will be used, and with whom it will be shared.

- o **Data Minimization:** IoT solutions should only collect data necessary for the specific function of the device. Reducing the amount of personal and sensitive data collected minimizes privacy risks.

IoT Regulations and Compliance

With the increasing amount of data generated by IoT devices and the potential risks to privacy and security, governments and regulatory bodies have implemented various regulations to ensure that IoT systems are safe, secure, and compliant with legal standards.

1. **General Data Protection Regulation (GDPR)**

   - o **Overview:** The GDPR, enacted by the European Union in 2018, is one of the most comprehensive data protection regulations. It sets strict guidelines on how personal data should be collected, stored, and processed, with a focus on protecting individual privacy.

o **Impact on IoT:** IoT companies operating in or interacting with EU residents must comply with GDPR requirements, such as obtaining consent for data collection, providing transparency on data usage, and allowing users to request access to or deletion of their data.

o **Key Requirements:**

   ▪ **Data Minimization:** Only the minimum necessary data should be collected from IoT devices.

   ▪ **Right to Erasure:** Users have the right to request that their data be deleted from systems.

   ▪ **Data Breach Notification:** IoT companies must notify users and regulatory bodies of any data breaches within 72 hours.

2. **California Consumer Privacy Act (CCPA)**

   o **Overview:** The CCPA, which came into effect in 2020, is a data privacy law in the state of California, USA. It gives California residents greater control over their personal data, including the right to know what data is being collected, request data deletion, and opt-out of data sales.

- o **Impact on IoT:** IoT companies targeting California residents must comply with CCPA regulations, including transparency in data collection and usage and providing users with the option to control their data.
- o **Key Requirements:**
    - **Right to Access:** Users can request a copy of the personal data collected by IoT devices.
    - **Right to Opt-Out:** Users can choose to opt-out of the sale of their data to third parties.
    - **Data Deletion Requests:** Users can request the deletion of their personal data held by the company.

3. IoT Cybersecurity Improvement Act of 2020

- o **Overview:** In the United States, this act focuses on improving the cybersecurity of IoT devices by requiring manufacturers to implement basic security standards for connected devices.
- o **Impact on IoT:** The act mandates that IoT devices used by federal agencies meet specific security requirements, such as secure passwords,

patch management, and vulnerability assessments.

- o **Key Requirements:**
  - **Basic Security Standards:** IoT manufacturers must build security features into their products, such as secure boot, software updates, and the ability to change default passwords.
  - **Risk Assessments:** Manufacturers must conduct risk assessments to identify potential vulnerabilities in their devices.

4. Network and Information Systems (NIS) Directive

- o **Overview:** The NIS Directive is a European Union law that sets cybersecurity requirements for operators of essential services, including those in critical infrastructure sectors like energy, transport, and health, many of which rely on IoT technologies.
- o **Impact on IoT:** Organizations operating critical infrastructure must ensure that IoT devices are secure, protected against cyberattacks, and compliant with NIS cybersecurity requirements.
- o **Key Requirements:**
  - **Cybersecurity Risk Management:** IoT systems must be designed and operated

with cybersecurity in mind to prevent disruption of essential services.

- **Incident Reporting:** Companies must report significant cybersecurity incidents to authorities within a specified timeframe.

Ethical Dilemmas in IoT Development

As IoT technologies continue to evolve, they raise important ethical questions. Developers and companies must address these dilemmas to ensure that their IoT solutions are not only effective but also socially responsible and aligned with societal values.

1. **Data Privacy vs. Convenience**
   - **Dilemma:** Many IoT devices collect large amounts of personal data to improve functionality and user experience. For instance, smart home devices may collect data on user preferences, while wearable devices track health metrics. However, this data can be vulnerable to misuse or unauthorized access.
   - **Ethical Consideration:** The ethical dilemma lies in balancing the convenience of personalized

services with the need for privacy protection. Users may willingly share their data for convenience but may not fully understand the extent of data collection or potential risks.

- o **Solution:** Developers must prioritize user consent and transparency. Clear privacy policies and easy-to-understand terms of service should be provided, ensuring that users are aware of what data is being collected and how it will be used.

2. **Surveillance and Personal Freedom**

- o **Dilemma:** IoT devices like smart cameras, microphones, and GPS trackers can be used to monitor activities for security or convenience. However, they can also be used for surveillance, raising concerns about personal freedom and privacy.

- o **Ethical Consideration:** The ethical concern is whether the use of IoT devices crosses the line into unnecessary surveillance, infringing on individuals' right to privacy.

- o **Solution:** Developers should implement strict controls over data access, ensuring that data is only used for its intended purpose and is securely stored. Clear user controls should be implemented to allow users to manage their privacy settings and deactivate devices if needed.

3. Bias in AI-Driven IoT Systems

- **Dilemma:** Many IoT systems integrate AI and machine learning algorithms to automate decisions, such as in predictive maintenance or personalized recommendations. However, these systems can unintentionally introduce bias, especially if the data used to train algorithms is incomplete or unrepresentative.

- **Ethical Consideration:** The ethical concern is whether biased algorithms could lead to unfair outcomes, such as unequal treatment of individuals or groups.

- **Solution:** Developers must ensure that the data used to train AI models is diverse, representative, and free from bias. Regular audits and testing should be conducted to identify and mitigate any biases in the system.

4. Environmental Impact of IoT Devices

- **Dilemma:** IoT devices often require significant energy to operate, and the growing number of connected devices could increase energy consumption and contribute to electronic waste.

- **Ethical Consideration:** The ethical concern here is the environmental impact of producing and disposing of IoT devices, especially in the face of growing e-waste and energy demands.

249

o **Solution:** Developers and manufacturers should focus on creating energy-efficient devices and promoting sustainability through environmentally friendly materials and responsible recycling programs. Additionally, IoT solutions should be designed to reduce power consumption and increase device longevity.

Ethical and legal considerations in IoT are complex and multifaceted. As IoT continues to evolve, it is crucial for developers and businesses to consider privacy, security, regulatory compliance, and the potential societal impacts of their solutions. By addressing these concerns head-on, we can ensure that IoT technologies contribute to a safer, more equitable, and more sustainable future.

CHAPTER 26

IOT BUSINESS AND INNOVATION

Business Models Around IoT Solutions

The Internet of Things (IoT) has opened up new avenues for businesses to innovate, create value, and tap into new revenue streams. Various business models are being adopted to leverage IoT's capabilities to solve problems, streamline operations, and enhance customer experiences. Understanding the right business model for an IoT solution is crucial for its success and scalability.

1. **Product-as-a-Service (PaaS) Model**
   - **Overview:** The Product-as-a-Service model involves offering IoT-enabled products as a service rather than as a one-time purchase. In this model, businesses sell access to the functionality of IoT devices rather than the physical devices themselves. For example, a smart thermostat company could charge a subscription fee for access to its cloud-based service that adjusts home temperatures based on user behavior.
   - **Example: Nest** (now owned by Google) uses a similar model by offering smart thermostats as

part of a broader service platform that includes ongoing software updates, maintenance, and cloud-based analytics. Customers pay for the service, not just the device.

o **Benefits:** This model generates recurring revenue streams and allows businesses to maintain ongoing relationships with customers, providing opportunities for upselling and cross-selling additional services.

2. **Data Monetization**

o **Overview:** IoT devices generate vast amounts of data, which can be monetized by selling insights or aggregated data to third parties. Companies can leverage this data to offer analytics, predictive models, or trend forecasting to other businesses in their ecosystem.

o **Example: Waze**, a GPS navigation app, collects traffic data from its users to offer real-time traffic updates. Waze monetizes this data by selling insights to local businesses for targeted advertisements or traffic planning.

o **Benefits:** Data monetization can create a new revenue stream for businesses while adding value to their IoT solutions. However, it is essential to ensure user consent and transparency when collecting and selling data.

252

3. Subscription-Based Business Model

- **Overview:** The subscription-based model involves offering IoT products and services as part of a subscription package. For example, a company might provide a smart home solution that includes hardware (IoT devices) and ongoing software and service updates for a monthly fee.

- **Example: Ring**, a home security company, provides a subscription service that offers cloud storage for recorded video footage and advanced features like motion detection alerts. Customers pay a recurring fee for access to these features and services.

- **Benefits:** This model ensures steady cash flow through predictable, recurring payments and allows businesses to maintain customer relationships and offer continuous value through software updates, service improvements, and ongoing support.

4. IoT as a Platform (IoTaaS)

- **Overview:** The IoT as a Service (IoTaaS) model allows businesses to offer IoT solutions through cloud-based platforms, where customers can deploy, manage, and monitor IoT devices without the need to handle the technical infrastructure. This model is often used in sectors like smart cities, logistics, and agriculture, where scalability and flexibility are essential.

- o **Example: Amazon Web Services (AWS)** offers IoTaaS through **AWS IoT Core**, a platform that allows businesses to connect devices, store data, and analyze information in the cloud, providing a flexible and scalable solution without investing in infrastructure.
- o **Benefits:** This model reduces the upfront costs for customers, allows for rapid scaling, and provides businesses with the flexibility to offer solutions that can be tailored to a wide range of use cases.

5. Freemium Model

- o **Overview:** In the freemium model, businesses provide basic IoT services for free but charge for premium features. For example, a fitness tracker app may offer basic health tracking features for free but charge for advanced analytics, personalized coaching, or integration with other platforms.
- o **Example: Fitbit** offers a freemium model for its app, providing basic features for free but charging users for premium services like more detailed health insights, sleep analysis, and coaching.

254

    o **Benefits:** The freemium model allows businesses to attract a large user base while monetizing premium features. It is ideal for businesses aiming to increase user engagement and expand their customer base before implementing a paid tier.

How IoT Is Driving Innovation in Various Industries

IoT is fostering innovation across a wide range of industries by enabling new business models, improving operational efficiencies, and enhancing customer experiences. Below are examples of how IoT is transforming different sectors.

1. **Healthcare**
   - **Overview:** IoT is revolutionizing healthcare by enabling remote monitoring, personalized care, and more efficient hospital operations. Wearables, sensors, and connected medical devices are allowing healthcare providers to track patients' vital signs in real-time, improving patient outcomes and reducing healthcare costs.
   - **Innovation Examples:**
     - **Remote Health Monitoring:** IoT devices like smartwatches and fitness trackers monitor heart rate, sleep

255

patterns, and physical activity. These devices can send real-time data to healthcare providers, enabling early detection of potential health issues.

- **Smart Medical Devices:** Connected medical devices like insulin pumps and smart inhalers automatically adjust to the patient's needs, improving treatment outcomes.

o **Impact:** IoT enables more efficient healthcare delivery, reducing the need for hospital visits and enabling proactive care.

2. **Manufacturing**

o **Overview:** IoT is driving innovation in manufacturing through automation, predictive maintenance, and real-time monitoring. IoT sensors embedded in machines help manufacturers track performance, predict failures, and optimize production schedules, leading to improved efficiency and reduced downtime.

o **Innovation Examples:**

- **Predictive Maintenance:** Sensors monitor the condition of machinery, detecting anomalies and predicting when maintenance is needed. This reduces costly downtime and extends equipment life.

- **Smart Factories:** Connected machines in smart factories communicate with each other to optimize workflows, adjust production rates, and ensure optimal resource utilization.

o **Impact:** IoT helps manufacturers improve productivity, reduce costs, and streamline operations.

3. **Retail**

o **Overview:** In retail, IoT is enabling personalized shopping experiences, real-time inventory management, and automated customer service. IoT sensors and devices collect data on customer behavior, inventory levels, and store conditions, helping retailers make more informed decisions.

o **Innovation Examples:**

- **Smart Shelves:** Retailers use smart shelves equipped with RFID tags and sensors to track inventory levels in real-time. This allows for automatic restocking and reduces out-of-stock situations.

- **Personalized Shopping Experiences:** IoT-enabled devices in retail stores can track customers' movements and preferences, allowing for targeted promotions and personalized recommendations.

- o **Impact:** IoT is reshaping the retail landscape by improving supply chain efficiency and creating more personalized and seamless customer experiences.

4. **Agriculture**

- o **Overview:** IoT is driving innovation in agriculture by enabling precision farming. IoT sensors monitor soil moisture, weather conditions, and crop health, helping farmers optimize irrigation, fertilization, and pest control.

- o **Innovation Examples:**
  - **Smart Irrigation Systems:** IoT sensors in the soil monitor moisture levels and automatically adjust irrigation schedules, ensuring optimal water usage.
  - **Livestock Monitoring:** Wearable IoT devices track the health, location, and activity of livestock, enabling farmers to detect illness and improve herd management.

o **Impact:** IoT helps farmers increase crop yields, conserve resources, and improve operational efficiency.

5. **Transportation and Logistics**

o **Overview:** IoT is transforming transportation and logistics by enabling real-time tracking of shipments, vehicles, and goods. IoT solutions help logistics companies optimize routes, reduce fuel consumption, and improve delivery times.

o **Innovation Examples:**

- **Fleet Management:** IoT sensors in vehicles track location, fuel usage, and maintenance needs. This helps fleet operators optimize routes and schedule maintenance.

- **Smart Logistics:** IoT-enabled containers and packages can be tracked in real-time, providing visibility into the supply chain and improving inventory management.

o **Impact:** IoT is making transportation more efficient, reducing costs, and improving the overall supply chain experience.

Real-World IoT Business Case Studies

1. **Case Study 1: John Deere – IoT in Precision Agriculture**

   o **Overview:** John Deere, a global leader in agricultural equipment, has integrated IoT into its machinery to enable precision farming. The company's machines are equipped with IoT sensors that provide real-time data on crop conditions, soil moisture, and equipment performance.

   o **Outcome:** The IoT-enabled machinery allows farmers to optimize planting, irrigation, and harvesting, improving crop yields while reducing water and pesticide use. John Deere has successfully adopted a subscription-based business model for its IoT-enabled services, including data analytics, machine health monitoring, and precision farming tools.

2. **Case Study 2: Amazon – IoT in Logistics and Retail**

   o **Overview:** Amazon has leveraged IoT to optimize its logistics and retail operations. The company uses IoT devices in its warehouses and distribution centers to monitor inventory, track packages, and manage orders.

- o **Outcome:** IoT has helped Amazon automate its supply chain, improve delivery times, and offer personalized recommendations to customers. The company's Amazon Go stores use IoT sensors and computer vision to create a cashier-less shopping experience, where customers simply pick up items and leave without checking out manually.

3. **Case Study 3: Tesla – IoT in Electric Vehicles**

- o **Overview:** Tesla has incorporated IoT into its electric vehicles to provide real-time monitoring and diagnostics. The vehicles are equipped with sensors that track battery health, vehicle performance, and driver behavior.

- o **Outcome:** Tesla's IoT-enabled vehicles receive over-the-air software updates, allowing for continuous improvement of features like autopilot and energy efficiency. The company's business model includes selling connected services, such as autonomous driving features, to enhance customer experience and create additional revenue streams.

IoT is reshaping business models and driving innovation across multiple industries. From product-as-a-service to data monetization and subscription-based models, businesses are finding new ways to leverage IoT for sustained growth and value creation. As IoT continues to evolve, its impact will only grow, creating new opportunities for businesses to innovate and engage with customers.

CHAPTER 27

CONCLUSION AND LOOKING AHEAD

Recap of Key Takeaways

Throughout this book, we've explored the fascinating world of the **Internet of Things (IoT)**, from its foundational components to the future trends that will shape its evolution. Below is a summary of the key takeaways:

1. **Understanding IoT**: The Internet of Things is the network of physical devices embedded with sensors, software, and other technologies that enable them to connect, collect, and exchange data. IoT is not just about connecting devices but also about enabling them to interact with the world, process data, and make autonomous decisions.

2. **Components and Architecture**: We examined the various components of an IoT system, including **sensors**, **actuators**, **devices**, **network protocols**, **cloud and edge computing**, and **data storage and analytics**. Understanding these components and how

they interact is crucial for designing, deploying, and maintaining IoT systems.

3. **Security and Privacy**: Given the sensitive nature of the data IoT devices collect, ensuring **security and privacy** is paramount. Data encryption, secure authentication, and robust regulatory compliance (e.g., GDPR, CCPA) are all essential elements to building secure IoT systems that protect users' information.

4. **Business Models and Innovation**: IoT is not only a technological revolution but also a business revolution. From **subscription-based models** to **data monetization** and **IoT as a Service (IoTaaS)**, businesses are finding innovative ways to generate value through IoT solutions. These business models are driving growth in industries like **healthcare**, **manufacturing**, **retail**, **agriculture**, and **smart cities**.

5. **Future Trends**: The future of IoT is exciting, with advancements in **5G**, **AI**, **blockchain**, and **edge computing** poised to drive new use cases and opportunities. As more devices become connected, IoT will enable smarter cities, personalized healthcare, autonomous vehicles, and much more,

revolutionizing industries and improving the quality of life.

6. **Challenges and Ethical Considerations**: As IoT continues to expand, challenges related to **scalability, data management**, and **ethical concerns** will remain. Ensuring that IoT technologies are used responsibly and ethically, with a focus on privacy and security, will be critical to their successful adoption.

IoT's Impact on the Future of Technology

The impact of IoT on the future of technology cannot be overstated. As IoT continues to evolve, it will play an increasingly important role in transforming the world in the following ways:

1. **Smart Cities**: IoT will make cities smarter and more sustainable by optimizing traffic, reducing energy consumption, and improving public services. IoT-enabled sensors will allow cities to monitor air quality, waste management, water usage, and infrastructure health in real time, leading to better urban planning and resource management.

2. **Healthcare Revolution**: IoT will significantly improve healthcare by enabling continuous patient monitoring, reducing hospital visits, and providing real-time data for early diagnosis and treatment. Wearables, connected medical devices, and remote patient monitoring will become mainstream, allowing for more personalized and preventative care.

3. **Industrial Automation and Efficiency**: In industries, IoT will drive **Industry 4.0** by automating manufacturing processes, optimizing supply chains, and enabling predictive maintenance. Sensors and smart machines will communicate with each other to improve production efficiency, reduce waste, and enhance product quality.

4. **Autonomous Systems**: IoT will be a cornerstone of **autonomous vehicles**, drones, and robots. These systems rely on IoT devices and sensors to navigate, make decisions, and interact with their environment, leading to safer and more efficient transportation, delivery, and service industries.

5. **Personalized Experiences**: IoT will enable personalized experiences in sectors like **retail**, **entertainment**, and **hospitality**. By collecting data

266

on user preferences and behaviors, businesses can create tailored services, recommendations, and interactions that enhance customer satisfaction and engagement.

6. **Environmental Monitoring and Sustainability**: IoT will contribute to **environmental sustainability** by enabling smart energy grids, efficient water management, and monitoring of environmental conditions. These technologies will help reduce carbon footprints, conserve resources, and provide early warnings for natural disasters.

Final Thoughts on Becoming an IoT Professional

As IoT continues to revolutionize industries and everyday life, the demand for skilled IoT professionals will continue to rise. Becoming an expert in IoT offers exciting opportunities and challenges in a rapidly growing field. Here are some key considerations for anyone interested in pursuing a career in IoT:

1. **Develop a Strong Foundation in Core Technologies**: To succeed as an IoT professional, it's essential to have a solid understanding of key IoT

components such as sensors, connectivity protocols, cloud computing, and data analytics. Gaining expertise in **hardware design**, **network architecture**, and **software development** will give you a comprehensive understanding of how IoT systems function.

2. **Stay Updated on Emerging Technologies**: IoT is evolving rapidly, and new technologies like **5G**, **edge computing**, **blockchain**, and **artificial intelligence (AI)** are transforming the landscape. Keeping up-to-date with these advancements will allow you to stay ahead of the curve and identify innovative solutions in IoT applications.

3. **Learn About Security and Privacy**: As an IoT professional, you'll need to understand the ethical and legal aspects of working with IoT systems. Focus on **cybersecurity** principles, **data protection laws**, and **privacy regulations** to ensure that the IoT systems you build or manage are secure and compliant.

4. **Hands-On Experience**: IoT is a practical, hands-on field. Engage in projects that allow you to build and experiment with IoT devices and platforms. Work on real-world problems, such as developing IoT

solutions for **smart homes**, **industrial automation**, or **healthcare**, to apply your skills and gain practical experience.

5. **Collaboration and Cross-Disciplinary Skills**: IoT projects often involve cross-disciplinary collaboration between engineers, software developers, data scientists, and business professionals. Strong communication and teamwork skills will be critical to successfully working in IoT development teams and bringing IoT solutions to market.

6. **Understand Industry-Specific Applications**: Different industries have specific IoT use cases, from healthcare and agriculture to manufacturing and retail. Specializing in a particular sector can enhance your value as an IoT professional, as you'll understand the unique challenges and opportunities within that industry.

The Internet of Things is one of the most transformative technological trends of the 21st century, and its impact on our world will only continue to grow. Whether you're an entrepreneur, engineer, or business professional, there's never been a better time to get involved in the IoT space. The future of technology is interconnected, and IoT will be at the heart of this transformation.

We've covered a broad range of topics throughout this book, and I hope you now have a deeper understanding of IoT's potential and the opportunities it presents. Whether you're just starting your IoT journey or looking to enhance your expertise, the knowledge gained here will be valuable as you navigate the world of connected devices and smart systems.

Good luck in your journey to becoming an IoT professional, and I look forward to seeing how you contribute to the exciting world of IoT innovation.

www.ingramcontent.com/pod-product-compliance
Lightning Source LLC
LaVergne TN
LVHW051439050326
832903LV00030BD/3160